Praise for
Get Out of Your Own Way

- "Powerful, practical insights that can help many to live more rewarding lives—turning weaknesses into strengths. *Get Out of Your Own Way* to achieve more satisfaction in yourself and all your intimate relationships. Goulston & Goldberg show us specifically how to convert problems into opportunities. A rewarding, clear and pleasurable book."

  —Harold Bloomfield,
  author, *How to Survive the Loss of a Love*

- "*Get Out of Your Own Way* treats this sensitive subject with rare kindness and common sense. The sincere reader will benefit by learning that they are not alone in the ways they self-interfere and will treat themselves with greater kindness and understanding."

  —Tim Gallwey,
  author, *The Inner Game of Golf*

- "Busy entrepreneurs don't have the time or energy to waste on feeling bad. This book can help you quickly confront and solve problems that get in the way of your success."

  —Jane Applegate,
  author, *Jane Applegate's Strategies for Small Business Success*

(continued)

- "This book offers down-to-earth insights and no-nonsense exercises to overcome your self-defeating behaviors and get on the road to the health and happiness you deserve."

—Kathy Smith,
America's leading health and fitness expert

- "This is a valuable book. It provides clear insight, compassionate understanding and practical solutions to forty self-defeating behaviors which can destroy your life if left unaddressed. Use it as a manual to free yourself from a self-imposed prison and create the life you truly want."

—Jack Canfield,
coauthor, *Chicken Soup for the Soul*

GET OUT OF YOUR OWN WAY

Overcoming Self-Defeating Behavior

Mark Goulston, M.D.,
and
Philip Goldberg

A Perigee Book

A Perigee Book
Published by The Berkley Publishing Group
A division of Penguin Putnam Inc.
375 Hudson Street
New York, New York 10014

First edition: February 1996

The Penguin Putnam Inc. World Wide Web site address is
http://www.penguinputnam.com

Published simultaneously in Canada.

Library of Congress Cataloging-in-Publication Data

Goulston, Mark.
Get out of your own way : overcoming self-defeating behavior /
Mark Goulston and Philip Goldberg. — 1st ed.
p.   cm.
"A Perigee book."
ISBN 0-399-51990-4
1. Self-defeating behavior.   2. Self-management (Psychology)
I. Goldberg, Philip.   II. Title.
BF637.S37G68   1996
1588.1—dc20   95-22993
                                                        CIP

PRINTED IN THE UNITED STATES OF AMERICA

20   19   18

*In loving memory of
Irving Goulston, Ideal Stotsky
and
William McNary*

Contents

*10 Things You Can Learn from Self-Defeating
       Behavior*   xi

Introduction: How to Beat Self-Defeat   xv

1. Chasing After Love and Approval From
       a Parent   1

2. Getting Involved With the Wrong People   6

3. Procrastinating   11

4. Expecting Others to Understand How
       You Feel   15

5. Waiting Until It's Too Late   21

6. Getting So Angry You Make Things Worse   25

7. Saying Yes When You Want to Say No   29

8. Holding a Grudge   33

9. Assuming They Don't Want Anything
       in Return   37

CONTENTS

10. Playing It Safe   41

11. Always Having to Be Right   45

12. Focusing on What Your Partner Is
    Doing Wrong   49

13. Putting up With Broken Promises   54

14. Trying to Make up While You're Still Angry   59

15. Not Learning From Your Mistakes   63

16. Trying to Change Others   67

17. Rebelling Just for the Sake of Rebelling   71

18. Talking When Nobody's Listening   75

19. Pretending You're Fine When You're Not   79

20. Becoming Obsessive or Compulsive   83

21. Taking Things Too Personally   88

22. Acting Too Needy   92

23. Having Unrealistic Expectations   96

24. Trying to Take Care of Everybody   100

25. Refusing to "Play Games"   104

26. Putting on an Act to Make a
    Good Impression   108

27. Being Envious of Others   113

28. Feeling Sorry for Yourself   117

29. Assuming the Hard Way Is the Right Way   122

30. Thinking "I'm Sorry" Is Enough   126

31. Holding It All In   130

32. Quitting Too Soon   135

33. Letting Others Control Your Life   139

34. Leaving Too Much to Chance   143

35. Letting Fear Run Your Life   148

36. Not Moving on After a Loss   152

37. Not Getting Out When the Getting Is Good   156

38. Not Asking for What You Need   161

39. Giving Advice When They Want
Something Else   166

40. Backing Down Because You Don't
Feel Ready   171

Acknowledgments

Much appreciation and gratitude are owed to John Duff for his persistent faith in this book; to Lynn Franklin for her generous efforts on its behalf; to Eric and Maureen Lasher for their early support and advice; and to Erika Schickel for her clerical help. For their ongoing encouragement, I am indebted to my colleagues Drs. Edwin Shneidman, Herbert Linden and Judd Marmor; to Michael Cader, Mark and Mia Silverman, Preston Johnson, Vicki Martin, Doug Kruschke, Brooke Halpin, Julie Turkel, Alan Duncan Ross and Marilyn Kagan; and to my mother, Ruth Goulston. To my wife, Lisa, and our children, Lauren, Emily and Billy, thanks for your understanding and tolerance of the time this book took away from you. And for their inspiration, thanks to all the patients who never gave up hope that they would overcome their self-defeating behavior.

10 Things You Can Learn from Self-Defeating Behavior

Since this book was first published, I have been extremely gratified by the response I've received from readers. I have also learned a great deal from those readers—and from the reaction to my "Top Ten" lists of things we can learn from the self-defeating behavior of public figures, from O.J. Simpson to President Clinton, which I've written for various publications. Thanks to the insightful readers who have applied the advice in this book to their lives, I have come to realize that there are universal lessons to be learned from understanding the nature of self-defeating behavior. Therefore, to help you get even more out of this book, here are the Top Ten Lessons I've Learned From Readers.

1. *Work on it now.* One of the greatest tragedies you can experience is to come to the end of your life and realize that it has not been everything you'd hoped it would be. Even more tragic is to realize that your failure to fulfill your hopes and dreams was due in large part to your inability to get out of your own way. It's never too late. The time to overcome your self-defeating behaviors is *now*. Otherwise, you run the risk of suffering deep regret over opportunities missed, satisfaction lost, and love not given or received.

2. *Jump from the frying pan onto the counter, not into the fire.* In your haste to change a self-defeating behavior, make sure you don't just substitute a *different* self-defeating behavior. The new one might even be more damaging than the original. Remember, if you shoot from your hip you can end up shooting yourself in the foot. Acting rashly in an effort to find a new coping mechanism can provide momentary relief only to complicate your life, damage your credibility, and end up making you hate yourself for acting foolishly. Instead of waiting until a similar situation arises and acting impulsively, figure out in advance what course of action would provide a lasting solution, not just a temporary substitution.

3. *Avoidance is no solution.* In an attempt to change a self-defeating pattern within a relationship, some people decide to avoid trouble by keeping their feelings to themselves. Staying angry and living with the pain seems to be a better choice than having another argument. The problem is, if you do not deal with hurt and disappointment quickly enough those feelings harden into resentment, anger, and hate. They fester inside and eventually turn into physical symptoms and/or emotional powder kegs. In the long run, it's much less self-defeating to acknowledge the problem early on and deal with it effectively—with compassion, respect, and empathy.

4. *There is nothing more futile than trying to change another person.* In an attempt to take the easy way out, some people try to change others rather than work on their own self-defeating behavior. "Hey, I wouldn't lose my temper if she stopped criticizing me!" "I wouldn't have to criticize him if he wasn't such a slob!" When it's so difficult to change yourself, how on earth do you imagine that it

will be a simple task to change someone else? You are better off concentrating on overcoming your own self-defeating behaviors and changing yourself for the better. As for the other person, they're much more likely to come around if you use understanding and acceptance rather than coercion and guilt.

5. *You can't fix something until you admit it's broken.* A fine line separates being direct from being blunt, being assertive from being abrasive, being strong-minded from being stubborn, being sensitive from being histrionic, or being spontaneous from being impulsive. Knowing the difference means recognizing the truth about your behavior, which is the first step to positive change.

6. *It takes seconds to destroy trust and years to rebuild it.* The longer you persist in self-defeating behavior the more likely you are to lose the respect and trust of others. Even if no one is immediately hurt or offended by your actions, they will still become wary of what might happen next—and it can take a long time to earn back their respect and trust. So get on with it before the road back to respectability becomes too long to travel and all the sympathy you're used to getting turns to pity. The longer you avoid changing, the more your friends will avoid you.

7. *Where there's a way, there's a will.* Studies show that people stay in unsatisfying jobs and relationships because they can't find a *way* to change that feels right, makes sense, and is doable. Simply having the will is not enough. You also need a way. And in fact, sometimes the way precedes the will. Visualize a practical alternative to your self-defeating behavior. Then, when you find yourself starting down the rocky road to self-defeat, pause, reflect, and replace the destructive behavior with the more constructive way of dealing with the situation.

8. *You* can *teach an old dog new tricks*. Often, the main obstacle to change is a lack of confidence that you can actually learn and implement new approaches to old problems. To avoid making the commitment to grow, we sometimes look for flaws in every new idea and find a reason to reject them. That's why, for instance, some people use the fact that computers sometimes crash as an excuse for keeping cumbersome paper files. They're actually afraid they won't be able to work the computer.

9. *Self-involvement is usually at the root of self-defeating behavior in relationships*. It's great to work on your self-defeating behavior, but don't get so obsessed that you lose sight of those who matter to you. The more preoccupied you are with yourself, the less likely you are to consider, acknowledge, or even notice other people. As a result, they feel hurt, frustrated, and angry—convinced that you don't really care about them. That's no way to keep a friend or lover. You can begin to repair such rifts only through empathy. Get in the habit of putting yourself in the other person's shoes by asking yourself, "What is it like for him/her right now?"

10. *Few things make you feel worse than giving in to self-defeating behavior, but few things make you feel better than overcoming it*. Like eating sweets or having an affair, the high you feel after indulging in self-defeating behavior is short-lived. And the shame, guilt, and self-contempt you feel in their wake is not only chilling but long-lasting. But if you nip self-defeating behavior in the bud, resist the temptation to give in to it and replace it with a positive *self-developing* behavior, you will discover more self-esteem and self-respect than you have ever experienced in your life.

Introduction:
How to Beat Self-Defeat

In 1972, after two grueling years in medical school, I was on the brink of dropping out. My class work felt oppressive, and I could not decide on a specialty because none of them appealed to me. What I liked was spending time with patients. I was moved by their suffering, and found that I had a natural inclination for calming them and easing their concerns. But, in an age of high-tech medicine, spending time talking to patients and alleviating their anxieties was considered lightweight. It was mere handholding. Doctors did hard work, heroic work, battling with death. I became so concerned about this dilemma, in fact, that I developed chronic stomach problems.

My mentor, the dean of students, arranged for me to participate in a program at the Menninger Foundation for Psychiatric Education and Research in Topeka, Kansas. I viewed it as a chance to be in a less pressured environment and sort out what I wanted to do. I got much more than I bargained for. After several weeks in the psychiatric wards, talking and listening to numerous patients, I thought for the first time of specializing in psychiatry. The work came easily and naturally to me.

But, for that very reason, I resisted it. In my mind, work was not supposed to be something you enjoyed but something you endured. If it wasn't hard, it wasn't legitimate.

I told all this to the dean. He thought the answer was simple: become a psychiatrist.

"But that would be the easy way out," I protested.

His reply changed my life: "Sometimes the easy way out is the right way in."

The experience not only influenced my choice of careers but the way I subsequently practiced it. It made me vividly aware of the power of self-defeating behavior. I had come close to defeating myself in two ways that would later become chapters in this book: quitting too soon and assuming that the hard way is the right way. I was saved by a caring person whose wise words had an immediate impact and continued to guide me when I ran into obstacles. "Sometimes the easy way out is the right way in" is what I call a usable insight: a memorable phrase that not only illuminates but inspires constructive action.

Since then, I have spent more than two decades in clinical practice. I have tried to identify how my patients are defeating themselves and to give them the empathy and usable insights they need to beat self-defeat. This book was written to help readers like you do the same. It will enable you to change the patterns that have held you back and turn your behavior from self-defeating to life-enhancing.

THE IMPACT OF SELF-DEFEATING BEHAVIOR

In my experience, self-defeating behavior is the main reason people go to psychotherapy. Nothing drives us crazier—or makes us hate ourselves more—than to realize we've been keeping ourselves from gaining the love, success and happiness we want in our lives. That's what self-defeating behavior does. It works against our own best interests. It defies our deepest desires. It creates more problems than it solves. That's why, when you catch yourself at it, you want to scream in exasperation, "I can't believe I did that again! I should have known better! I'm my own worst enemy!"

How many times have you said those words to yourself? Chances are, your answer is "Too often!" How many times have you identified exactly how you're defeating yourself and vowed never to do it again? Too often? Relax. The first thing you should know is that you're not alone. My patients have ranged from ordinary folks struggling to make ends meet to powerful tycoons who could buy and sell the rest of us; from the young and healthy to frail patients on their deathbeds; from the obscure to the famous; from honest citizens to hardened criminals. Every one of them has felt foolish because of self-defeating behavior, and every one has been unable to figure out how to change—or, if they did know how, failed to follow through. In some cases, people who exuded confidence and self-assurance on the outside were

plagued by so much self-contempt that they felt unde-
serving of love and respect.

One of my patients was a world-renowned jazz musician. During the last months of his life, as terminal cancer dragged him slowly toward death, he was a tormented
soul. Obviously, self-defeating behavior had not kept him
from being successful; he was one of the most revered
instrumentalists of his time. But some of the behaviors
covered in this book had kept him from enjoying his success, from holding onto love and from finding peace
when it mattered most. By holding a grudge, he had deprived himself of the love of his son; by waiting until it
was too late, he was unable to make peace with the son
before he died; because he envied others—in his case,
classically trained musicians—he could not fully appreciate the esteem in which he was held; because he had
unrealistic expectations, he bemoaned the fact that the
sound from his instrument matched perfectly the music
in his head only four times in his career (which was four
more perfect moments than most of us achieve); and by
holding it all in, he could not unburden himself of his
deepest feelings.

The last words I spoke to him were, "Let it go, you
did good." He smiled weakly and his eyes watered.
"Thanks, Doc," he said. "I needed that." I'll never know
if it made a difference.

This book was written to help avert such tragedies. If
you are ready for change, it will help you find the conviction and direction to follow through. By following the
advice in the chapters ahead, you will find that instead of
defeating yourself you will be able to face difficult situations with dignity, wisdom, courage and even humor.

WHY WE DEFEAT OURSELVES

Self-defeating behavior occurs when we fail to learn the lessons that life tries to teach us. It represents the victory of impulse over awareness, immediate gratification over lasting satisfaction, relief over resolution. Self-defeating behavior invariably begins as an attempt to make ourselves feel better. It is a coping mechanism. When faced with a crisis, a threat or a potentially upsetting situation, we try to protect ourselves. We grasp for something that will reduce tension or keep us from getting hurt. The action itself seems logical and expedient at the time, and it might actually succeed in bringing about short-term relief. But that behavior invariably comes back to haunt us. Then we curse ourselves for being stupid, foolish or weak, when in truth we had simply lost perspective in the midst of a threatening or confusing situation.

As with most persistent patterns, self-defeating behavior usually has roots in childhood experience. When children confronted with traumas are given both loving support and patient, effective guidance, they tend to develop healthy coping mechanisms. As adults they tend to be resilient, confident and resourceful. Any self-defeating behaviors they have are relatively minor and easy to overcome. By contrast, children who are not loved, and are abused or neglected instead, feel unprotected and alone. Then there are children who do not lack affection and attention, but are not given adequate guidance. Although they might feel loved, they often grow up feeling incompetent and incapable, and therefore unsafe in the face of adversity. In either case, they reach for anything they can find to make their unbearable feelings bearable. The more anxious and alone or inadequate and incompetent they feel, the more tenaciously they hold to whatever thoughts, attitudes and behaviors bring relief. If they do not develop more effective coping mechanisms, the ones that bring relief solidify into self-defeating behaviors.

Naturally, there are fortunate individuals who, because of inherent strengths or the intervention of other adults, develop adequate ways to cope despite the lack of parental love and guidance. In most cases, however, they end up with stubborn self-defeating behaviors. People who were abused as children tend to get angry and strike out at the world. People who were neglected tend to feel defeated and withdraw from the world. People who were not given guidance tend to lack confidence and self-reliance. Each pathway leads to different forms of self-defeat.

HOW TO USE THIS BOOK

> *"All the beautiful sentiments in the world weigh
> less than a simple lonely action."*
> —*JAMES RUSSELL LOWELL*

Each of the forty concise chapters in the book addresses a common self-defeating behavior. If you read through the titles in the table of contents, you will no doubt recognize the ways you defeat yourself. Some will seem more relevant than others. But I suggest that you read the book straight through, from beginning to end, then go back and focus on the chapters that relate to your present concerns. Study them carefully and follow the advice they contain.

After this initial phase, I suggest you keep the book handy as a reference source. There are two reasons for this. First, as new situations arise, you might, like most people, find new ways to defeat yourself. Different chapters will suddenly take on new meaning and new importance. Second, you might need a refresher course from time to time; self-defeating behaviors have a way of cropping up long after you thought you'd seen the last of them. Positive changes in behavior have to be practiced repeatedly before they become second nature.

Each self-defeating behavior has its own character and its own solutions. At the same time, they have various features in common. Therefore, certain countermeasures are effective in every case. Whenever you find yourself in a situation that has, in the past, triggered a self-defeating impulse, follow these steps in addition to the recommendations in individual chapters:

The Five-Step Pause

Self-defeating behaviors are usually knee-jerk reactions. We act without regard for long-term consequences and without considering reasonable alternatives. The Five-Step Pause is designed to prevent that by increasing awareness. It is a way of returning your mind to the loop, allowing you to be reflective instead of reflexive, to act on intelligence instead of on impulse and consciously choose the best course of action.

Step 1: Increase physical awareness. Impulses begin

as physical sensations. Stop and notice what you feel and where you feel it. In your stomach? Head? Neck? Chest?

Step 2: Increase emotional awareness. Try to connect the physical sensation to an emotion. Why do you feel tense? What do you feel angry about? What are you afraid of?

Step 3: Increase impulse awareness. Do the feelings you just noticed make you want to take action? What do they make you want to do?

Step 4: Increase consequence awareness. Ask yourself what the outcomes are likely to be, in the short run and the long run, if you take that action. Becoming conscious of the undesirable consequences of that action serves as a deterrent.

Step 5: Increase solution awareness. Ask yourself what alternatives you have. Which of those is likely to produce the best outcome? Picturing the good things that will happen if you act more constructively can serve as an incentive to change.

Focus on What You're Gaining, Not What You're Losing

No matter how destructive it is, a self-defeating behavior serves a purpose. And no matter how much you want to stop doing it, on some level you might be afraid of leaving it behind in favor of something new and untested. You wonder, what if the new behavior doesn't work and things get worse? For that reason, a key to breaking the inertia is to shift perspective from what you're giving up to what you're gaining. Otherwise, even after you have made a solid commitment to change, you can easily revert to your self-defeating ways as soon as you run into an obstacle.

Get Some Help

Since self-defeating behavior goes back to the childhood experience of being alone and defenseless, it is easier to overcome it in adulthood if you get support from other people.

The actual role your helpers play doesn't matter. They can assist you directly, provide moral support or agree to hold you accountable for the changes you vow to make. What's important is that you know you're not alone. This will strengthen your confidence and determination.

Use Setbacks Constructively

Self-defeating behavior usually repeats itself. Despite your best intentions, when the same or similar situations crop up again, you might act reflexively and do what you've done before. If you have a setback, instead of beating yourself to death for making a mistake, convert your self-contempt into self-determination. Ask yourself what you would do if you could do it over again. Develop a plan of action for the next time the situation arises.

Reward Yourself

Each time you repeat a self-defeating behavior, you suffer a blow to your self-esteem. You see yourself as weak and undisciplined, unable to follow through on your higher intentions. On the other hand, each time you successfully overcome a self-defeating impulse, you gain a measure of self-respect. Take advantage of that feeling of pride. Rewarding yourself for a job well done will reinforce your new behavior and help you make the change permanent.

Refer to the Usable Insight

> *"That is what learning is. You suddenly
> understand something you've understood all your
> life, but in a new way."*
> —DORIS LESSING

Ordinary insights provide relief and better understanding, but they don't necessarily spark action. *Usable* insights have a more practical and lasting impact. My patients find that the insights in this book inspire constructive change and remain in their minds long after they first hear them. One patient called them "the gift that keeps on guiding." I recommend that you write down the insights that pertain to the behaviors you are working on and post them on the bathroom mirror or refrigerator door. The reminders will reinforce your new course of action.

> *"If you create an achievement, you create a habit.
> If you create a habit, you create a character.
> If you create a character, you create a destiny."*
> —ANDRÉ MAUROIS

THE COMMITMENT TO CHANGE

This book will give you the inspiration, knowledge and skills to stop undermining yourself. But none of it will help if you are not committed to change. The mere fact that you've read this far suggests that you have the necessary courage. It's not easy to admit that you get in your own way, and harder still to take responsibility for getting out of your way. You have realized that blaming your problems on other people, or on circumstances beyond your control, doesn't make anything better. You understand that you alone have the power to change your life. That sense of responsibility is crucial if you're going to beat self-defeat.

I urge you to remain steadfast in your commitment to improving your life. Look at yourself candidly as you proceed with the book. As they say in Twelve-Step programs, "make a searching and fearless moral inventory." Your honesty, combined with the information and advice in each chapter, will give you the confidence and wisdom to leave self-defeating behavior behind and move forward to a more satisfying future. Instead of being your own worst enemy, you will become your own best friend.

1

Chasing After Love and Approval From a Parent

"Children begin by loving their parents; as they grow older they judge them; sometimes they forgive them."
—OSCAR WILDE

A patient of mine told her mother she was seeing a therapist. "Terrific," sniffed the mother. "He'll try to convince you that you hate me."

"No, Mom," replied my patient. "I knew that going in. He's trying to convince me that I love you."

That story comes as close as anything to capturing the complex feelings between adult children and their parents. Almost everyone I see in therapy has conflicts with a mother or a father, and these invariably affect their relationships with spouses, offspring, colleagues and friends. Some are angry because they feel deprived of parental approval or love. Some are frustrated because their parents don't understand them and won't even try. Some resent their parents' attempts to control them, while others resent their indifference. And almost all of them feel guilty for not appreciating those who sacrificed so much to raise them. As time slips away they become increasingly anxious. It's no wonder so many attempts to get what they need turn out to be self-defeating.

Because of your parents' own upbringing, they are often incapable of giving you what you need emotionally. If you keep chasing after what they can't give, and if you make your sense of worth dependent on getting it, you will never feel worthwhile. Instead, your futile efforts will create animosity and resentment in you and frustration in your parents. Actually, unless you are the rare son or daughter who articulates your needs clearly, your parents probably don't even have a clue as to what you want from them. All they know is that you're displeased—and that bewilders and saddens them.

In many cases, what you do not get from your parents is precisely what your parents never received from their own. Because it is hard for them to give what they haven't received, they end up mimicking their own upbringing or perpetuating the deprivation in other ways. The key to breaking the family cycle is: act as your parent's parent, in essence becoming your own grandparent. Give to your parents what they never got. By tapping into their hidden yearning, you might just free them to give you what you need.

> *"The joys of parents are secret, and so are their
> griefs and fears."*
> —*FRANCIS BACON*

Carolyn, a 50-year-old client, had a meddlesome mother who always disapproved of her daughter's choices. "She won't stop treating me like a child," Carolyn complained. "I want to cut her off, but I just can't do it."

Carolyn wanted what we all want from our parents—unconditional love and acceptance—but her desperate attempts to get it had the self-defeating effect of distancing her from her mother. I reminded Carolyn that her mother had been raised during the Depression by parents who were forced to work long hours. Like other neglected children, Carolyn's mother grew up feeling ignored. Hence, when she became a mother herself, she went overboard, becoming so involved in her daughter's life that she tried to control it. "The sad thing about both of you," I told Carolyn, "is that neither of you really had a mother."

When she realized that she and her mother had both suffered in childhood—her mother from being neglected, she from being overly controlled—Carolyn was able to let go of some of her bitter feelings. Realizing that her mother's controlling nature was a misguided attempt to be close to her daughter allowed Carolyn to be more receptive. The less she pulled away, the less her mother pushed. Before long, her mother's critical comments ceased. Instead of yelling, the two women began to talk to, and eventually with, each other. Their three remaining years turned out to be sweeter than the previous fifty.

This insight works especially well for men who long to hear their fathers say the magic words, "I'm proud of you, son." Men who, as kids, did not have the admiration of their dads feel a gaping deprivation; those who *did* have it long for sweet boyhood moments they can never recapture. That is why, if you want to see a grown man cry, get him to talk about his father.

One memorable patient, a rock star I'll call John, had driven himself to succeed, largely in an effort to win his dad's approval. But nothing—not the gold records, the money, nor the acclaim—could get his father to express his pride directly. I advised John to be his own grandparent, but he was too proud to act on the insight. Then his father had a stroke. John was called upon to help care for him. After a few days of nursing this once strong man, the son's heart began to soften. As he helped his father dress for his seventy-sixth birthday, John said, "Well, another year older, another year wiser."

"Another year older anyway," sighed his father.

John was stunned. His father had never uttered a self-deprecating word in his life. As he watched him struggle with his shoelaces, John recalled that the old man had been raised by siblings and had been more deprived of paternal affection than John himself. When his father finished tying his laces, John said, "Nice going, Dad, I'm proud of you."

The father's eyes welled with tears. He whispered words that meant more to John than a roomful of Grammy Awards: "I'm proud of you, too. You're a good son."

> *"First we are children to our parents, then parents to our children, then parents to our parents, then children to our children."*
> —MILTON GREENBLATT, M.D.

It takes courage to be your own grandparent. You have to be willing to give what you might sorely need yourself, with no guarantee of a return. However, it might be your best hope for getting the love, pride and acceptance you have always wanted. At the very least it will help prevent the anguish that a patient of mine expressed so well: "What eats away at me is not the love I didn't get from my mother, but the love I never got to give because I was so angry."

USABLE INSIGHT:
If you want what you never got from your parent, become your own grandparent.

TAKING ACTION

- Think of something you never received from one of your parents, and that you feel you still need. (The most common responses are pride, love, comfort and acceptance.)
- From your knowledge of your family, determine whether your parent is likely to have received it from his or her parents.
- Imagine a specific situation in which you could sincerely give it to your parent, and visualize yourself doing so.
- Seek opportunities to offer what you need to your parent. Don't be surprised if both of you are moved, even to the point of tears. The tears don't mean something is wrong, but that something that *was* wrong has finally been made right.

2

Getting Involved With
the Wrong People

*"Be courteous to all, but intimate with few, and
let those few be well tried before you give them
your confidence."*
—GEORGE WASHINGTON

"Maybe I should become a nun!" Judy proclaimed as she plopped into the chair. "I just broke up with another guy. It started out great, but he turned out to be a domineering bastard. The total opposite of the wimp I was with before, the one who couldn't even decide what restaurant to go to. Why do I always get involved with men I end up feeling scared of or sorry for? Isn't there some way to spot them in advance?"

Judy is not the only one who wishes she had some sort of jerk detector. And it's not just women who have this wish. Men complain that the women they're attracted to turn out to be either bitchy and controlling or needy and clingy. And both sexes complain about friends, family members and colleagues who either attack them constantly or crumble at the slightest offense.

Like shoppers trying to spot bad apples without taking a bite, we wish we could identify the rotten people because, unlike rotten apples, *they* bite *us*. If you repeatedly get involved with the wrong people, each of them is probably one of two types. The first type impresses you with power, charisma and strength. If you feel powerless, you might be drawn to one of them in hopes of absorbing some power by osmosis or association. The irony is that, like vampires, these people sustain their power by sucking it from others. They are takers. You might not realize this because they know how to make you feel special. That's because they haven't started to hurt you yet. They will before long.

You're drawn to people of the second type because they need you. You identify with them, and treat them as you want to be treated. It's a chance to do good, to feel important, or even be a hero. They seem unthreatening, incapable of hurting you. But they are also incapable of giving much. You feel that if you prop them up enough, they will eventually be capable of giving something back. More often than not, they simply drain you. In the long run, you feel used and used up, and you become exactly what you never wanted to be: cold, aloof and maybe even abusive to them.

With both types, your best intentions defeat you in the end. One way to avoid this outcome is to identify the core of the other individual's personality. This enables you to relate more effectively instead of wishing you'd never met the person. Those to be wary of have either a core of hate or a core of hurt.

People with a *core of hate* are at war with the world. Often charming at first, they are competitive, adversarial and usually belligerent. They turn every disagreement into a confrontation and quickly try to gain the upper hand. When you're with them, you end up feeling wrong or inferior.

"A true friend unbosoms freely, advises justly,
assists readily, adventures boldly, takes all
patiently, defends courageously, and continues a
friend unchangeably."
—WILLIAM PENN

Often the products of abusive childhoods, people with a core of hate can't stand to lose. It's as if they were so badly hurt as children they vowed to always get their way as adults. You might welcome such combativeness from your lawyer, but not from friends, lovers or associates. You can become so afraid of getting hurt that you sacrifice your own needs to accommodate them.

Tell a core-of-hater your goals and aspirations, and he will try to deflate your enthusiasm and maybe even root against you. Watch him in the company of someone less fortunate than himself, and he tends to be unconcerned, perhaps even scornful or condescending.

People with a *core of hurt* are more frustrating than hurtful. Being with them is like walking on eggshells; unless you're extra careful not to hurt their feelings, you'll end up feeling guilty. They take everything personally, but instead of lashing out they fall apart and retreat, making you feel sorry for them.

Usually products of emotional neglect, core-of-hurters grow up feeling unloved, unspecial, unprotected, and unworthy. They won't root against you, but they won't root *for* you either. They simply feel too deprived to root at all. Around the less fortunate they feel too depleted and overwhelmed to help; then they feel inadequate because they can't rescue the person.

*"A noble person attracts noble people, and knows
how to hold on to them."*
—GOETHE

Fortunately, there is a third type: those who have a *core of health*. Open-minded, confident, with strong convictions and a good sense of humor, they are the ones we want in our lives. Made to feel safe and loved as children, core-of-healthers tend to be loyal, honest and sincere. When hurt or upset, they bounce back quickly, without holding a grudge or trying to even the score. Because they are not threatened by anyone else's success, they will root for you with enthusiasm. With the less fortunate, they are genuinely compassionate and usually try to help. These are the people to turn to in times of need.

Unfortunately, most people you meet will have either a core of hate or a core of hurt. It's not necessarily self-defeating to associate with them, unless you get pulled into their core like a beam of light into a black hole. If you handle them effectively, you might be able to build a satisfying relationship. Just remember, changing is *their* responsibility, not yours.

USABLE INSIGHT:
Avoid the core of hate, understand the core of hurt, seek out the core of health.

TAKING ACTION

How to Deal With a Core of Hate
- If you can't avoid them, accept that you can't change them.
- Don't become too intimate or trusting.
- Don't get suckered into competing with them. You can't win with people who won't lose; even if you gain a victory they won't let you enjoy it.
- Don't be intimidated or get deterred from acting in your own best interests.
- Don't argue or debate with them; just think of a fair and reasonable course of action, and follow through.

How to Deal With a Core of Hurt
- Understand that just because they act hurt doesn't mean you're hurting them.
- Don't get trapped in their moods or take responsibility for cheering them up.
- Remember, it is not in your power to make them happy.
- Try to deal with them dispassionately and objectively.
- Clarify ahead of time which behaviors and attitudes you expect of them, and what they can reasonably expect of you.

3

Procrastinating

*"It is better to begin in the evening than
not at all."*
—ENGLISH PROVERB

*"Procrastination is the art of keeping up
with yesterday."*
—DONALD ROBERT PERRY MARQUIS

*"Loneliness . . . is and always has been the central
and inevitable experience of every man."*
—THOMAS WOLFE

At a seminar, I asked an audience of 500 men and women to raise their hands if procrastination ranked among their top three self-defeating behaviors. Almost 90% did.

Nearly everyone puts off until tomorrow what could be done today, even experts on self-defeating behavior. For years, every time I was quoted in the media, people would say, "You should write a book." It was flattering, but it made me feel awful. I *knew* I should write a book. I *wanted* to write a book. I had even started one. But there was always a reason to put the work off. I mocked myself: "How can you help people change when you can't even conquer your own laziness?"

Then I realized what was holding me back. I was *lonely*. The prospect of long, intense periods of working alone seemed intolerable. Once I recognized the problem, I knew what to do: find a partner and collaborate. From that point on, the book came together smoothly and enjoyably.

There are, of course, many reasons people procrastinate: self-doubt, boredom, fear of failure, the feeling of being unready or unprepared and so on. But these feelings, by themselves, don't necessarily lead to procrastination. Often what tips the scales is going through them alone, with no one to help you, bolster you, or cheer you on. You might curse yourself for being lazy, or cowardly, or lacking in confidence, but your real obstacle might be loneliness, especially if you procrastinate mainly on solitary tasks.

The problem usually has early roots. For example, when a child takes her first tentative steps toward walking, she fluctuates between the thrill of mastery and the terror of the unknown. When she feels thrilled, she doesn't need anyone. But as soon as she becomes frightened, she looks back to her mother or father to restore her sense of safety and boost her confidence. Hearing "It's okay, don't be afraid, you can do it!" helps her move forward. But if she looks back and does not find that support, she will fall down and revert to crawling. She will not be ready to walk as long as she has to do it alone. The process is similar each time a child has to face a difficult task. If no adult is there to offer comfort and support, the child will come to associate challenges with the pain of being alone.

A child who is given encouragement, guidance and

reassurance will grow up to have the adult counterparts—confidence, common sense and resilience—to call upon in times of doubt. On the other hand, if solitary pursuits trigger emotional memories of being vulnerable and afraid, he will tend to procrastinate as an adult.

The key to overcoming loneliness-based procrastination is to enlist the support of other people.

A procrastinator can become an activator when he's around others. That's why people have jogging buddies, study groups and collaborators. It is also why successful self-help groups like Alcoholics Anonymous rely on "sponsors" to help struggling members through difficult times.

In the absence of a full partner, try to involve someone who will bolster your efforts. I did this, for example, with a woman who had delayed work on her Ph.D. dissertation for three years. I phoned her every morning at nine o'clock and asked her questions such as, "Are you at your desk? What are you going to do next? What will you do when that's finished?" I also had her leave me a message each time she completed another hour of work. It might seem unnecessary to treat a responsible adult this way, but it worked. Like most of us, she didn't mind putting up with some duress as long as she did not have to endure it alone.

If you can't find an actual partner or monitor, try conjuring the image of a loving parent, grandparent, friend or teacher—someone you would not want to disappoint, and whom you can imagine saying, "Good work, you're doing great!" when you finally do what you've been avoiding. Even if only imagined, the support of another person can be the key to getting done what you would otherwise put off.

USABLE INSIGHT:
We procrastinate not because we're lazy, but because we're lonely.

TAKING ACTION

- Stop wasting more time putting yourself down for procrastinating.
- Stop setting yourself up by saying, "Next time it's going to be different."
- Arrange to work with a partner.
- Or, enlist the aid of a supportive friend and check in with him or her when you are struggling to begin a task.
- Reciprocate by offering to help the friend with something he or she is trying to get done.

4

Expecting Others to Understand How You Feel

*"No human being can really understand another,
and no one can arrange another's happiness."*
—GRAHAM GREENE

A 42-year-old historian, Janet Lake had taken a sabbatical from her university to write a textbook. To balance her isolation, she set up frequent get-togethers and accepted every invitation that came along. She complained that she had to practically beg her husband, Robert, to join in. Robert viewed the pressure as an invasion of privacy, and belittled Janet's "excessive need to socialize." Janet also griped that when her husband *did* join in, he was rude and unfriendly. In return, Robert criticized her for being "hypercritical."

By the time the Lakes came to see me, the issue threatened to destroy their seven-year marriage. Clearly, each spouse had valid feelings and felt entitled to be understood. Just as clearly, neither one could comprehend the other. The gap was so huge they might have hailed from separate planets. To make things even more tense, each was convinced that the other *could* understand but just didn't want to.

"You don't understand!" is one of the most frequent accusations hurled between people. It's exasperating to be misunderstood, so we explain ourselves again and again. And again. Then the frustration escalates to anger, because even more upsetting than not being understood is feeling that the other person isn't even *trying* to understand. Our feelings are perfectly obvious to us, so they must be obvious to them too. They're just being stubborn. They don't care! So we try to force them to understand, which makes them feel cornered, and now there are two angry people. If they weren't in the mood to understand before, they're certainly not now.

> *"The human understanding is like a false mirror, which, receiving rays irregularly, distorts and discolors the nature of things by mingling its own nature with it."*
> —FRANCIS BACON

It's important to realize that because we filter reality through individual values and perceptions, misunderstandings are inevitable; at times it is impossible to comprehend another person's thoughts or emotions. However, it *is* possible to feel what someone else is feeling.

Deep down, each of us has the same fundamental need for love, affection, esteem, security, self-expression and other basics. When those needs are thwarted we feel anger, fear, sadness, pain, and other universal emotions. By focusing on such commonly experienced feelings, you can achieve something deeper and more meaningful than understanding: empathy. Empathy is a priceless commodity because it invariably defuses hostility. *It is psychologically impossible to be angry at someone if, at the same time, you feel what he or she is feeling.*

One effective way to stimulate empathy is to use analogies to translate one person's feelings into the language of the other. To begin the process with the Lakes, I presented Robert with a hypothetical situation related to his position as the head of a design group in an engineering firm: "How would you feel if you were involved in a major project and someone on your team was sullen and flippant around your clients?"

Robert admitted that he would feel resentful and perhaps humiliated because his colleague's behavior might tarnish his own reputation. With some prodding, he was able to see the parallels to his wife's experience. Janet took pride in her reputation for bringing people together and stimulating conversation. In her eyes, Robert's curt behavior reflected badly on her and threatened a valued aspect of her life. Because friendships were as important to her as business relationships were to Robert, his antisocial behavior made her feel exactly the way he said he would feel in the imagined scenario. When Robert got the point, his posture visibly softened. "I'm sorry," he said.

The Lakes were halfway to mutual empathy; now Janet had to feel what her husband was feeling.

It had become clear to me that Robert resisted socializing because he was more comfortable with objects and numbers than with people, especially strangers. By trivializing social events and acting as if Janet had no right to expect him to participate, he was able to conceal his sense of inadequacy and justify not making an effort.

To help Janet empathize, I evoked a subject about which she was equally sensitive—her skills as a parent: "Suppose every time you took your kids to day care, they behaved obnoxiously in front of others. Suppose no matter what you did, they would still misbehave." Janet said she would be mortified. She would feel so inadequate that she might avoid being seen with her children to spare herself the embarrassment—just as Robert needed to avoid company because he felt inadequate socially. Then, to help her empathize with her husband's bitterness about being criticized, I asked how she would feel if her own mother were to scrutinize her parenting and comment on her shortcomings. "I'd get nervous and flustered, and I'd resent it like hell," she admitted. Which was exactly what happened to Robert at gatherings.

It would be an exaggeration to suggest that analogies healed the Lakes' relationship. It did, however, change the atmosphere from one of antipathy to one of empathy. They now stood on calm, common ground and could discuss their differences like adults.

> *"The end of understanding is not to prove and find reasons, but to know and believe."*
> —THOMAS CARLYLE

While this process can be used whenever misunderstandings arise, it is especially helpful in male–female relationships. In that context, I have found certain types of analogies to be especially fruitful: for men, career situations and the need for autonomy; for women, relationship issues and the need for intimacy. As a general rule, regardless of their professions, status or expressed values, men and women tend to look to those areas for identity and respect. For a man, losing a job might elicit feelings of unworthiness similar to those of a woman whose love affair has ended. The frustration of a man trapped in a dead-end job is comparable to that of a woman hemmed in by children and household duties. A man's fear of humiliation is similar to a woman's fear of abandonment.

Feeling is more powerful than meaning. If you are willing to make the effort to feel what others are feeling—and to help them feel what you feel—you can use analogies to create empathy.

USABLE INSIGHT:
When they just don't understand, get them to feel
what you're feeling.

TAKING ACTION

- If not being understood has made you frustrated, instead of becoming hostile, pause and try to express yourself in a different way.
- Instead of lecturing, criticizing or intellectualizing, try using analogies that will help the other person feel what you feel.
- First, identify your emotions. Figure out exactly what you are feeling and why.
- Think of a situation that would make the other person feel what you feel. Analogies work best when

they fit the individual's personality and circumstances.

- Ask how he or she would feel in that situation. Don't
be accusatory; speak in an even, conciliatory tone.
- Once the other party acknowledges the appropriate
feelings, ask if he or she can see a parallel to your
experience. You might have to prod, as in, "When
you criticize me in front of our friends, I feel just the
way you do when . . ."
- Switch roles by imagining a situation in which you
would feel what the other person has been feeling.
- Let the other person know that you understand how
he or she feels. You are likely to see the hostility dis-
solve before your eyes, freeing both of you to communicate more openly.

5

Waiting Until It's Too Late

"If a man in the morning hear the right way, he may die in the evening without regret."
—CONFUCIUS

In 1991, my colleagues and I witnessed what I call the Michael Landon Malibu Epidemic. When that strong, virile actor developed terminal cancer, the thought "If it can happen to him, it can happen to me" spread like a virus. Suddenly, doctors and psychotherapists were flooded with phone calls.

Unfortunately, it often takes a tragedy to make us look honestly at our lives. Tragedies trigger reevaluation and regret, sometimes too late to make things right. Perhaps the most common example is the driven man who invests most of his energy in his career. Then someone dies—usually a father, a mentor or a contemporary—or the man himself is felled by a stress-related disease. He realizes he would need an extra lifetime to get through the books he'd intended to read. His kids have grown up without his participation. He and his wife have not had an intimate moment in years. Now he sees the wisdom of the oft-repeated observation, "No dying man ever wished he spent more time at the office."

I have seen grown men and women weep like babies because a parent died before they could reconcile or forgive, or fully express their love and gratitude. One was a woman who had severed relations with a mother who had belittled and criticized her for most of her life. For the sake of her sanity, she avoided her mother for fifteen years. When she learned from a relative that her mother had died, she was surprised to find warm feelings welling up within her. For the first time, her thoughts were not dominated by anger. Instead, she was consumed by regret. "Cutting my mother out of my life was an empty victory," she said. "It kept away the hurt, but it also kept away any chance for a positive connection."

> *"I think I don't regret a single 'excess' of my responsive youth—I only regret, in my chilled age, certain occasions and possibilities I didn't embrace."*
> —HENRY JAMES

One of the most poignant moments of my life occurred during medical school, when I worked part-time at a nursing home. On the first floor, where the sickest patients lived, a man sat stooped in his wheelchair all day, muttering bitterly to himself. I looked at his chart and, to my astonishment, realized he was a famous state supreme court judge. I asked the head nurse why the man had no visitors. She replied that he had alienated everyone in his life.

Living upstairs was Mr. Bronstein, who had so much vitality and joie de vivre that I wondered why he was in a nursing home. He explained that his wife lived on the first floor. After emigrating to America, the couple had worked side by side as a tailor and a seamstress. They had struggled through the Depression and World War II, and had raised three children who had done them proud. His wife had had a stroke. She could no longer speak or control her urine or feces, and she did not recognize her husband. Yet every morning he cleaned her bed, bathed her and braided her hair. "People ask why I bother," he told me. "My answer is, 'What could be more important? She's my lifelong partner, and she would do it for me.' "

More than likely, Mr. Bronstein died without regret. I doubt if the judge was that fortunate. He had achieved greatness, but if asked whether he would have done anything differently, he probably would have replied as Ty Cobb reportedly did: "I would have made more friends."

You already know what's important, but you might have pushed it out of your awareness so as not to upset the status quo. If it takes a death or a life-threatening illness to wake you up, it might just be too late.

USABLE INSIGHT:
You don't have to wait for someone to die before you realize what's important.

TAKING ACTION

- Imagine yourself at age 80, looking back at your life.
- Ask yourself what it would take to make you feel you had lived a meaningful life.

- If you continue living the way you are, will you be able to say, at age 80, that everything important has been resolved and completed?
- What can you do differently, starting today, that will get you to where you want to be at 80?
- Start doing it.

6

Getting So Angry You Make Things Worse

"Anger is a short madness."
—HORACE

"No man can think clearly when his fists are clenched."
—GEORGE JEAN NATHAN

Marianne was the only woman on the writing staff of a TV show. Her gender had never been an issue; she was always treated as an equal. Then she took a maternity leave. When she returned to work, she found that her ideas were no longer taken seriously and her new assignments were beneath her level of skill and experience. It was as if, in her absence, she had been demoted.

The problem was compounded by Marianne's commitment to breast-feeding. Each time she excused herself briefly to pump milk into a container, one colleague would bellow, "Mooooo!" while the others made breast jokes. Marianne was enraged, but she knew that if she unloaded on her coworkers she would reinforce the stereotype of a hormonal female who can't fit in or take a joke. Losing her temper would also defeat her own purpose, which was to regain the respect she had long ago earned.

> *"Anger and folly walk cheek by jole."*
> —BENJAMIN FRANKLIN

Marianne was right, of course. You can gain momentary relief from venting your anger, but often at the risk of doing something you later regret, and losing the moral high ground in the bargain. The opposite choice—to suppress the anger—is equally dangerous, because the feeling will fester and perhaps lead to depression or psychosomatic illness. As I told Marianne, there is a third option: *convert the anger to conviction and act on the basis of principle.* Doing this arms you with the clarity, courage and strength to take effective action.

I advised Marianne to think about the principles that her colleagues were violating and find a way to stand up for them. At the next opportunity, she addressed the group: "I think we agree that we should all act professionally and treat each other as equals. So, if you think providing food for my child is an unprofessional distraction, I'll stop doing it . . . on one condition: you guys stop taking personal calls, talking about your dates, and interrupting meetings to talk about football. Tit for tat. No pun intended."

> *"I understand a fury in your words,*
> *But not the words."*
> —SHAKESPEARE

By acting from conviction, and adding a touch of humor, Marianne put a halt to the offensive behavior without sacrificing her dignity. Then she was able to address other issues—such as her diminished responsibilities—from a position of integrity and strength. Had she acted hurt or defensive, her grievances would have been discredited and she would have lost even more respect—probably even her own.

Whenever you can transcend your personal feelings and uphold strongly felt values, you gain something far greater than the thrill of retaliation: the courage and power of conviction.

USABLE INSIGHT:
Anger makes you wild, but conviction makes
you strong.

TAKING ACTION

Whether you're dealing with offensive colleagues, a stubborn spouse, a disobedient child or a brazen bully, here's how to convert anger to conviction:

- Cool off. Resist the urge to act impulsively, and take some time to reflect on the situation.
- Ask yourself what has made you angry. The answer is usually something you regard as unfair or unreasonable.

- Identify the principles that are being violated, and put your conviction into words.
- Determine the best and most creative way to stand up for your principles.

7

Saying Yes When You Want to Say No

*"My unhappiness was the unhappiness of a
person who could not say no."*
—DAZAI OSAMU

When Becky and Ann agreed to write a book together,
Becky could not have been happier. Ann was not only a
published writer but her best friend. Becky bought a
computer and set up an office in her spare bedroom, and
the new partners got to work.

Immediately, a pattern was established. Ann set the
agenda and dominated the sessions, pacing the room like
a mad genius who could not contain her bustling imagination, while Becky sat at the keyboard and typed. When
something tedious had to be done, Ann assumed that
Becky would do it. When Ann asked Becky a question,
she sounded as though she were speaking rhetorically to
a subordinate, not soliciting the opinion of an equal.
Becky's own ideas were routinely discounted or ridiculed.
She came to dread their work sessions.

Ann's behavior was inappropriate; Becky's was self-
defeating. She was so afraid that Ann would cancel the

project that she could not assert herself. At the same time, she could not go along with Ann's agenda without feeling resentful. By not saying "no," she was in effect saying "yes" and perpetuating her own abuse. Even more self-defeating was not discussing the situation and instead letting the anger and frustration build. Eventually, she erupted: "You treat me as if you're the boss and I'm your underling," she shouted. "You're an arrogant know-it-all!"

That ended the problem, all right. It also ended a promising partnership and a once-beautiful friendship.

Being unable to say "no" without fear or "yes" without resentment is a common dilemma. A breadwinner, for example, might fear that he will lose his family's affection if he were to scale back their spending. But if he doesn't, he might resent being taken for granted. People who live with substance abusers know that refusing to cooperate with the addiction can trigger an explosive outburst or a childish accusation. Yet, if they go along, they resent being manipulated.

If you find yourself in a situation where you resent acquiescing to unacceptable behavior but are afraid to oppose it, you might be tempted to simply avoid the person. Of course, that won't do if he or she plays a necessary role in your life. But neither would continuing on your no-win course. The only way out is just to say "Stop!" But, remember that timing is crucial. If you wait too long to speak up, the other person will feel offended and throw it back at you: "So, you've been holding this in all along. You're nothing but a phony!" Or, as Becky's former partner responded, "What am I, a mind reader? How am I supposed to know it bothered you so much?"

Had Becky acted before her frustration reached the breaking point, she might have avoided her outburst and instead said something like, "Maybe I should have spoken up sooner, but the way we work together upsets me. I realize you know more than I do, but I have something to contribute too, and it's frustrating when my ideas are not taken seriously. I hope that as we go along you'll be able to treat me more like a real partner."

The key is to notice the early warning signs of frustration, such as feeling less and less enthusiastic about seeing the other person, realizing that you're the only one who acts supportive, or feeling like a coward for giving in.

You don't have to go along when others act unfairly or unreasonably. If you *do* go along, make it clear that you are doing them a favor—and that you expect something in return.

USABLE INSIGHT:
When you can't say no without fear, or yes without resentment, it's time to say stop!

TAKING ACTION

- Realize that not wanting to go along doesn't make you stubborn, mean or defiant.
- Understand that not saying no can be taken as a yes, and can reinforce the unwanted behavior.
- Make sure you confront the person at an opportune time.

- Express your grievance as an observation.
- Speak in terms of how it hurts or frustrates *you*; don't be accusatory or judgmental.
- Admit your own participation in creating the problem.
- Say specifically how you would like the situation to be different in the future.
- Make it sound like a suggestion or request, not an ultimatum.

8

Holding a Grudge

"The weak can never forgive. Forgiveness is the attribute of the strong."
—*MAHATMA GANDHI*

"There is no revenge so complete as forgiveness."
—*JOSH BILLINGS*

"Forgive and forget" is one of those common sayings that sounds like good advice but is very difficult to live up to. Despite our best intentions, when push comes to shove, *not* forgiving and *not* forgetting is what we end up doing.

Not forgiving is often synonymous with continuing to blame. A powerful defense mechanism, blaming amounts to finding a target for your anger and frustration. It protects you from having to own up to your own shortcomings. However, making your problems someone else's fault leaves you in a passive position. It feels good to be exempt from responsibility, but it keeps you from taking steps to remedy your situation.

Similarly, not forgetting is the equivalent of continuing to remember. That too is a form of self-protection. You think that remembering a past hurt will keep you from letting your guard down, thereby protecting you from being caught unaware and getting hurt again. The problem is, your wariness can make you so uptight and guarded that others find it takes too much effort to deal with you. You could end up safe but alone. When is it safe to forget? When you have learned whatever you need to know to prevent a hurtful situation from recurring.

> *"To be wronged is nothing unless you continue to remember it."*
> —CONFUCIUS

Albert was an ambitious young executive with his eye on a position that was going to open up in his firm. During the time he was trying to impress his superiors and maneuver for advantage, he attended a company function with his wife, Sherry. An artist who danced to her own drumbeat, Sherry had too much to drink that night and embarrassed Albert with careless remarks. When someone else got the promotion he felt entitled to, Albert blamed his wife. For nearly a year, he attended social functions alone rather than risk embarrassment, and he reminded Sherry of the incident whenever he felt frustrated by the slow progress of his career. His continuing resentment threatened to destroy the marriage.

Then, at his annual review, Albert's boss told him exactly what had been holding him back and what he had to do to rise in the firm. Naturally, it had to do with his performance, not his wife. The reality check made him realize he had been wasting energy blaming Sherry. Eventually, as his work improved and his prospects brightened, he was able to forgive. Then he took the next step by rationally expressing his concerns to Sherry. She promised not to drink at company events and to respect the importance of appearance. When he was reasonably sure that the past would not repeat, Albert was able to forget as well as forgive.

> *"Forgiveness ought to be like a cancelled note—*
> *torn in two, and burned up, so that it never can*
> *be shown against one."*
> —*HENRY WARD BEECHER*

The best way to achieve forgiveness is to stop thinking about the grudge itself and focus on accomplishing important goals. If you push ahead and create a satisfying life, you will feel less frustrated and less angry. You will be more willing to take responsibility for your actions, and your need to blame will dissipate. You will not want to taint your happiness by being ungracious. In essence, getting ahead in your life will come to be more important than getting even.

The best way to forget is to improve your behavior and circumstances until you feel safe enough to let go of bitter memories. If someone has upset you in the past, try to work out an agreement with the person so you can feel reasonably sure it won't happen again. It's also a good idea to sort out what made you vulnerable in the first place and change your attitude or behavior. Knowing that you can handle a recurrence without being devastated will allow you to forget as well as forgive.

USABLE INSIGHT:
We forgive when we no longer need to blame; we
forget when we no longer need to remember.

TAKING ACTION

- Ask yourself what not forgiving and not forgetting is costing you.
- Acknowledge what the other person did wrong and what you would need from him or her in order to feel safe in the future.
- Ask yourself how *you* might have contributed to the problem.
- Determine what you need to learn to prevent a recurrence.
- Move on in your life. If you create a more fulfilling future, you will find it easier to forget the past.

9

Assuming They Don't Want Anything in Return

"Before borrowing money from a friend, decide which you need more."
—*ADDISON H. HALLOCK*

Hillary wanted very much to finish her graduate studies and become a psychotherapist. Low on money, she had been on sabbatical for three years, working for an accounting firm and taking whatever courses she could afford. Then she got lucky. Her sister and brother had a sudden business success and offered to pay for her schooling. "Just finish your training and be successful," they said graciously. "That's all the payback we want."

On the surface they were true to their word: Hillary was not expected to pay a penny in return. But she discovered she had accumulated other, more subtle debts. Suddenly, she was expected to travel cross-country for family functions, where she was clearly expected to mention at every opportunity how much she appreciated her benefactors. As her training progressed, her siblings would phone regularly to discuss problems with their children, spouses and each other. They were getting their money's worth in public displays of gratitude and free advice. They had been generous, but not entirely selfless. "If I'd have known what was expected of me, I'd have taken out a bank loan," said Hillary.

Hillary discovered the emotional equivalent of "There's no such thing as a free lunch." Consciously or unconsciously, nearly everyone keeps score of favors and gestures, and everyone is sensitive to being shortchanged. The strings attached can be exact equivalents, such as when you are expected to spend as much money on a birthday gift as was spent on yours. Other times the expectation is subtle—an extravagant display of gratitude, perhaps, or a change in behavior—and we end up feeling confused, betrayed and manipulated. If it happens often enough we can become cynical and adopt a hardened, "Don't do me any favors" attitude.

Why do we want to believe that people who give to us expect nothing in return? Because the desire for unconditional love springs eternal. We want to be given to just because we exist—as we had been or yearned to be as children, before we grew up and people started asking for something back. When people give to us and imply that they expect nothing in return (usually out of politeness), it evokes that childlike feeling of being cherished as something special. No wonder we want to believe it. That's why, when we discover there really are strings attached, we feel not only betrayed and angry but foolish for having deceived ourselves with a childlike wish.

When you accept someone's generosity, you might take on a debt you do not even know you owe, and if you fail to pay it back, you will be punished for reasons you cannot comprehend. To prevent this, it's a good idea to *assume* that a payback is expected. You can confirm this by saying to the giver, "I hope I'm in a position to do the same for you sometime." Even if they insist they want nothing, imagine what a fair payback would be and get ready to follow through, just in case. In general, it is safer to assume too much is expected rather than too little. Otherwise, you might think your debt has been repaid only to discover that it hasn't.

Try to determine at the outset whether the act is a gift, a favor or a loan. Each carries with it a different obligation. A gift requires at least a thank-you; a favor requires a similar action when your positions are reversed; a loan requires payment in kind.

Those distinctions are equally important when you are the giver. Don't kid yourself into thinking you are a saint who gives to others and wants nothing in return. If you are not clear about what you really expect, you can jeopardize relationships by seeing yourself as a victim. You might even withhold your trust and affection, and neither you nor the other person will know what has come over you.

USABLE INSIGHT:
There are always strings attached.

TAKING ACTION

• Assume that people always give with the expectation of receiving something in return, and don't become embittered by this realization.

- Determine whether the gesture is a gift, a favor or a loan.
- If it is a gift, be sure to express your gratitude, and perhaps find an occasion to offer a reciprocal gift or a display of thoughtfulness.
- If it is a favor, make a mental note to offer a favor in return.
- If it is a loan, spell out clearly how and when and with what you intend to pay it back.

10

Playing It Safe

"One doesn't discover new lands without consenting to lose sight of shore for a very long time."
—ANDRÉ GIDE

A man from a tribe in a nonindustrial culture was brought to New York City. Asked his impressions, he noted sorrowfully that everyone he saw on the street was looking down. "They don't see the sky," he said.

That observation captures what we miss out on when we don't take chances. The familiar expression "Look where you're going" makes sense if you are navigating the streets of Manhattan or driving on a freeway. It tells you to watch out for obstacles—good advice, but deadly if taken as a principle for living your life. It can make you overly cautious. You will slow down and maybe even lose your sense of direction entirely. Yes, there are situations in which it is better to be safe than sorry. But if you always play it safe, it's a safe bet you'll end up sorry.

Jonathan was a highly successful software designer in his late thirties. By all appearances he had an ideal life: a big home in Beverly Hills, a wife who was both beautiful and successful, two kids who made him proud, prestigious awards and a salary so big he was embarrassed when it was reported in the papers. But Jonathan was unhappy. Fourteen years earlier he had made a splash in Silicon Valley as a bold young innovator with daring ideas. When the early products he created became a huge success, he signed a long-term deal with a major company. Settled, secure and celebrated, he went on to manage a division that produced excellent products—but *safe* products. He had learned how to give consumers and stockholders what they wanted, but he was no longer bold and brash, and it bothered him. "I've lost my creative edge," he lamented. "I was a visionary. Now I'm a numbers guy."

> *"Whither is fled the visionary gleam?*
> *Where is it now, the glory and the dream?"*
> —*WILLIAM WORDSWORTH*

Jonathan had become good at looking where he was going, but he wanted once again to go where he was looking.

To look where you are going is to be motivated by fear; to go where you are looking is to be driven by desire, confidence and vision. If you know you can handle whatever cracks and bumps come along, you do not have to watch the pavement all the time. Instead, you can move full speed ahead with your eye on your goal.

The inclination either to play it safe or take risks can usually be traced to childhood. All children are adventurous and curious. If, when they get hurt or things go wrong, their parents respond angrily, as in, "Don't let me see you do that again," or fearfully, as in, "Don't do that or you'll get hurt," they are likely, as adults, to play it safe. When tempted to do something risky, their emotional memory whispers, "You'll be sorry." On the other hand, if their parents say, "Get back out there and try again," they usually grow up able to take risks for the sake of a dream.

> *"He has not learned the lesson of life who does not every day surmount a fear."*
> —*RALPH WALDO EMERSON*

Those who are comfortable taking chances know that the best way to grow is to reach beyond their grasp. Their sense of direction comes from the heart. They don't shy away from surprise; they might even seek it out. And they seldom die with regrets. In the end we regret not what we have done but what we have *not* done.

My friend Timothy Gallwey, author of *The Inner Game of Golf*, has his clients close their eyes to practice putting. He says it helps them develop a smoother stroke because they are forced to follow their instincts. In essence, that is what I tell patients who want to change the direction of their lives: close your eyes, get in touch with your inner vision, and start going where it leads you. You might stumble on occasion, but you will taste a lot more of life. And you will get to see the sky.

USABLE INSIGHT:
Don't look where you're going, go where
you're looking.

TAKING ACTION

- Think of yourself at a time in your life when you were optimistic and idealistic.
- Have this younger self take a critical look at your present self. Does he or she think you've been true to your dreams?
- Which of your unrealized dreams are still meaningful?
- Without being impractical, ask yourself what you can do now to get back on track. Or, what new vision would embody the feelings and experiences you once dreamed of having?
- Complete this sentence: "If I could change my life right now, I would _____."
- Try to turn your fears into opportunities. (When asked how he hit so many home runs, Sadahara Oh, the Japanese Babe Ruth, said he looked at opposing pitchers not as adversaries but as partners helping him to be a better hitter.)

11

Always Having to Be Right

*"It wasn't until quite late in life that I discovered
how easy it is to say 'I don't know!' "*
—SOMERSET MAUGHAM

*"Human beings are perhaps never more
frightening than when they are convinced beyond
doubt that they are right."*
—LAURENS VAN DER POST

A communications expert once made this distinction: "A know-it-all who doesn't know what he is talking about is a jerk. A know-it-all who *does* know what he is talking about is just an ass." Whether you know what you're talking about or not, it's self-defeating to act like a know-it-all.

Tom, an assistant managing editor at a magazine, came to see me when his life started caving in. First he was passed over for the promotion he coveted because, his superiors told him, he had "difficulty getting along with others." He was always talking down to people, they said. Then his wife filed for divorce. She called him an arrogant son of a bitch who always thinks he's right.

Tom had been raised by alcoholic parents who were frequently out of control and made their son feel wrong much of the time. As an adult, two needs dominated his interaction with others: to show he was right (along with the converse need to never be wrong) and to be in control at all times. In our first few meetings, I tried to engage him in a dialogue, or at least a discussion, but it invariably turned into a debate. I decided on a different strategy: to give him carte blanche to speak. After several sessions, he asked why I didn't interrupt him. "You seem to have a lot to say," I replied. Puzzled for a moment, he started to become belligerent, then lowered his head sheepishly and muttered, "Who am I kidding?"

By listening attentively and not challenging him, I had avoided what his know-it-all behavior was designed to provoke: a confrontation. Tom thrived on stirring things up so he could grab control. But he was a decent man, and it pained him to learn that people he loved and respected saw him as overbearing, self-righteous and disrespectful. Now that he had hit bottom, he was willing to look at himself more honestly.

> *"A man should never be ashamed to own he has been in the wrong, which is but saying, in other words, that he is wiser today than he was yesterday."*
> —ALEXANDER POPE

What he learned was this: like most people who have to be right all the time, Tom was acting out of self-defense. Deep inside, he believed the world was telling him, "You don't know what you're talking about." He wasn't trying to show that he was right so much as that he wasn't wrong. But his manner was so confrontational he came across as offensive, not defensive, as if he expected others to agree with, or defer to, his opinions. His message wasn't just "I'm not wrong" but "You *are* wrong."

If you act in self-defense when you're not being attacked, the *other* person will feel attacked. You won't be admired as a forceful person with strong opinions but resented as an opinionated bore. In a professional setting, if you're lucky enough to be exceptionally bright, talented or productive, people will tolerate your behavior. But they won't cut you any slack when it comes to making mistakes, they won't lend a helping hand because they either think you're not open to help or they want to see you fall on your face.

Unlike Tom, many know-it-alls never learn these lessons. After all, if you think you're always right you can't learn anything new. You're closed down because knowing and learning can't occur at the same time.

Having to be right all the time just isn't right. It isn't just, it isn't fair and it isn't even possible. It will bring you contempt, not power and esteem. On the other hand, being wrong on occasion does not make you less worthy, it makes you more human and more approachable.

USABLE INSIGHT:
When no one is attacking you, being defensive
comes across as offensive.

TAKING ACTION

- Next time you feel the need to show you're right, ask yourself if winning is important enough to risk hurting others and being resented.
- Look for feedback. If you're acting like a know-it-all, others will respond by either fighting back or acting defenseless and subdued—and then avoiding you.
- In proving you're not wrong, make sure you don't make others feel wrong.
- Recognize and acknowledge the value of other people's opinions and viewpoints.
- If you've offended someone, admit you were wrong. It's the best way to reconnect.
- Observe what it feels like to *not* be right. Can you handle the feeling? Remember, the reward is that you don't alienate people.
- Instead of being a know-it-all, strive to know all of it. Take into consideration the point of view of others and the requirements of the situation as a whole.

12

Focusing on What Your Partner Is Doing Wrong

"Let me be a little kinder,
Let me be a little blinder
To the faults of those around me,
Let me praise a little more."
—EDGAR A. GUEST

"A man never discloses his character so clearly as
when he describes another's."
—JEAN PAUL RICHTER

"Why should I bother trying? You're not willing to do a damn thing!"

"What? I'm the one who's making all the changes. I don't see you trying at all!"

That is a typical exchange in couples therapy. In an effort to reduce friction in a relationship, most of us are willing to do things to satisfy our partners even if they don't come easily—get rid of an annoying habit, for instance, or help with the chores, or try to hold our temper. Such changes can take considerable effort, but we are usually willing to try—if we think our partner is trying just as hard. But if our partner seems unwilling to match us effort for effort, we get resentful and try less hard ourselves.

Unfortunately, instead of focusing on our partners' attempts to improve the relationship, we tend to notice what they're doing wrong and what they're not contributing. Naturally, they respond with the same tunnel vision, and the cycle of resentment spirals downward until no one is appreciated and no one is doing the necessary work.

> *"If we had no faults of our own, we would not*
> *take so much pleasure in noticing those of others."*
> —FRANÇOIS, DUC DE LA ROCHEFOUCAULD

Like many couples, Ross and Nancy Koestler fought over money. Ross, who had grown up poor and worked his way into the middle class, accused his wife of being a reckless spender. Under pressure because business was stagnant, he questioned Nancy's every purchase and exploded if he thought she had been extravagant. Nancy, a freelance photographer raised in an affluent family, saw Ross as a tight-fisted man who would rather hoard money than allow himself or his family any pleasure. She felt hurt that he didn't trust her judgment.

Despite their problems, both spouses were committed to the marriage and were willing to work at it. Ross tried to control his temper and stop challenging his wife's spending. Nancy did her best to buy only necessities. But neither was able to recognize the other's efforts. "He's not doing a damn thing from his side," said Nancy. "Me?" Ross exclaimed. "I've been working on this marriage ever since we started therapy, but I don't see any change in you!"

Why are we so blind to our partners' efforts? For one thing, it's hard to keep score. When he forgets to clean up after a midnight snack, for example, the evidence is in the sink in the morning. But how do you keep track of the times he *does* clean up? Violations are not only easier to spot, but we deliberately look for them because they serve a purpose: they give us an excuse to cut back our own efforts. They also justify our anger. In long-term relationships, anger builds up over time, and we sometimes feel irate without an immediate cause. It's uncomfortable to be angry for no reason, so we look for evidence, like detectives searching for clues to justify a suspicion. Unfortunately, finding fault not only creates resentment, it keeps us from appreciating each other.

> *"Be quick to praise. People like to praise those who praise them."*
> —BERNARD BARUCH

It is far easier to work on a relationship if both parties focus on the other's efforts as well as their own. To help couples do this, I encourage them to answer the following questions. It helps them shift from disapproval to appreciation.

• What specific gestures have you seen your partner make to improve the relationship?

• Can you think of an incident where he did something on your behalf?

• Has she done anything she didn't really want to do just to make you happy?

• Has he held back from saying things you don't like?

• Has she controlled herself when she might have done something you can't stand?

• Has he tried to change a habit or behavior pattern that you've complained about?

To aid the process of developing appreciation, I also encourage couples to make their efforts concrete. Nancy Koestler, for example, promised to consult with Ross before making purchases over fifty dollars. Ross promised to control his temper and to put together a financial statement so Nancy could see exactly where they stood. In this way each spouse could keep track of the other's efforts.

Working at a relationship means doing what is in the best interest of two, even if it doesn't come naturally. To stick with it, we need to see our partner struggle as hard as we do. In the end, what counts is not what we do to each other, but what we do for and with each other.

USABLE INSIGHT:
If you really want to work on your relationship,
watch your partner's efforts, not just your own.

TAKING ACTION

• When you think your partner is not doing his or her share, ask yourself whether being resentful and fault-finding will help you or your relationship.

- Practice the Three A's: awareness, appreciation, acknowledgment:

  - Become aware of your partner's efforts. Try to notice the little things he or she does for the good of the relationship.
  - Appreciate that those efforts demand compromise and sacrifice—and that your partner loves you enough to try.
  - Acknowledge your partner's contributions. Don't keep your appreciation to yourself.

- After you establish a track record using the Three A's, you might find that your partner's behavior spontaneously changes. Sometimes people do things you don't like because they don't feel appreciated.
- If you still feel shortchanged by your partner's lack of effort, ask yourself if your objections are fair and reasonable.
- If they are, try to express any hurt and frustration you might feel without sounding critical.
- Tell your partner what changes you would like him to make. Ask if he thinks these changes are fair and reasonable, and if he is willing to make the effort.
- Ask him if there are any changes he would like to see you make.

13

Putting up With Broken Promises

"And be these juggling fiends no more believ'd,
That palter with us in a double sense;
That keep the word of promise to our ear
And break it to our hope."
—SHAKESPEARE

"We promise according to our hopes, and perform
according to our fears."
—FRANÇOIS, DUC DE LA ROCHEFOUCAULD

Broken promises are devastating because they clash with one of our deepest longings: to believe in other people. As helpless infants, we needed to trust our caretakers in order to feel safe; now, in adulthood, a broken promise can resonate with that early memory of vulnerability and make us angry, insecure, and sometimes as petulant as children.

What makes broken promises frustrating as well as painful is when promise-breakers don't own up to their misdeeds—often because they don't realize they made a promise in the first place. To make themselves feel comfortable, people will carelessly say things to ease your tension, soothe your worries, or, more selfishly, get you off their backs. They don't realize that you plan to hold them to their word. Hence, the boss hints at promotions to make employees feel secure, parents propose a trip to Disneyland to shut their kids up, and men allude to marriage to reassure their girlfriends and bask in the glow of adoration. In their minds, appeasing an awkward situation overrides the possible long-term consequences.

Sometimes we on the receiving end make it easy for promise-breakers by not holding them accountable. In order not to make waves, and to maintain their basic sense of trust, we rationalize the betrayal with "Oh, he just made a mistake," or "She must have forgotten." We do this because we are so frustrated that we are on the brink of exploding or imploding, and we're terrified of losing control. Unwilling to lose a friend or cause an ugly scene, we ease off and say it's okay, and eagerly accept their promise another time.

Making excuses for chronic promise-breakers is invariably self-defeating. If you don't admit how upset you are, or if you minimize the damage that has been caused, the promise-breaker will continue to be unconcerned about letting you down. And if later you confront him, he'll simply make excuses, knowing that you'll back down again—or he'll insist that he merely made a mistake rather than own up to having done something wrong.

If the commitment-breaker is a repeat offender, you will eventually find yourself cringing when he makes another promise. When this occurs, take it as a sign that you're burned out on excuses and it's time to draw the line. The first step is to ask yourself, "Am I frustrated beyond any hope of reconciliation? Is the relationship important enough to lower my expectations, or should I cut my losses now?"

If you choose to stick it out, you have to be prepared to hold the person accountable. Try to do it before you get so mad that you lose your cool, and try to raise the issue in a nonthreatening manner. An excellent way to stand up for yourself while avoiding a hostile faceoff is to use what I call the Columbo Defense. Like Peter Falk's famous TV character, you lean forward without making eye contact and scratch your head as if you are extremely perplexed. Then you say that, while you might be mistaken, you seem to remember that some kind of promise had been made. This is a disarming way to introduce a delicate subject when truth is on your side but you don't want to rub the other person's nose in it.

A patient of mine named Mandy used the method with her boyfriend Tom, who had a habit of letting business interfere with romance. Once, when he canceled a long weekend at a desert spa, Tom said, "I'll make it up to you. Next spring my schedule will be lighter and we'll go to Hawaii for a week." As spring edged toward summer with no trip in sight, Mandy grew increasingly annoyed. She couldn't let Tom get away with another broken promise, but she knew that if she lost her temper or expressed irritation he would get defensive and accuse her of being demanding.

Instead, Mandy used the Columbo Defense. One night, after a lovely dinner, she said to Tom, "You know, I'm kind of confused. Maybe my memory is off, but I believe you said that you were going to arrange a trip to Hawaii this spring. Do you remember that?"

Tom knew what Mandy really meant: "Okay, you made a promise. I'm not going to bitch about it, I'll just refresh your memory and give you a chance to get your act together." Her approach got his attention, commanded his respect, and gave him no way out except to lie blatantly. Best of all, it gave Tom a face-saving way to "remember" the promise and belatedly make good on it.

Habitual promise-breakers usually think they can get away with it. If you don't want to be a doormat, you have to let them know that betrayal exacts a cost. But be prepared to follow through; if they call your bluff and you cave in, you will be breaking an unspoken promise to yourself.

USABLE INSIGHT:
If they break too many promises, don't let them
make any promises.

TAKING ACTION

- When someone breaks promises repeatedly, try to make the next one binding, so you don't end up in a bind when it's time for the payoff.
- Clarify your expectations: "That sounds like a promise. If you don't come through, it's going to hurt. So, how much should I bank on it?"
- Don't bring up past offenses. It's a waste of time and possibly an invitation to a fight.
- Establish a time frame: "When can I count on this to happen?" If the person resists, set the deadline yourself: "I'll remind you of it on the first of the month."

- If the person does not follow through, pin him down in a nonthreatening way. Wit and imagination work better than confrontations or ultimatums.
- If diplomacy fails, let the person know the consequences of not keeping the promise. For example, say "I'll start dating other men," or "I'll have trouble trusting you again."
- If you follow these steps, the promise-breaker might turn into a promise-keeper. If there is no change, however, he probably has no intention of keeping his promises (as opposed to someone with good intentions who makes promises carelessly). You might not want to accept another promise from him.
- Practice what you preach. If you want people to keep their promises to you, make sure you keep yours. Making promises you can't keep is just as self-defeating as letting promise-breakers get away with it.

14

Trying to Make up While You're Still Angry

"Violence in the voice is often only the death rattle of reason in the throat."
—*JOHN FREDERICK BOYES*

Not long after I gained some notoriety as an expert on relationships, I found myself struggling with my own marriage. After a series of minor incidents, so much resentment had accumulated that my wife and I had become cold and hostile toward one another. At times I feared that I'd even stopped loving her. One night I lay in bed ruminating while she read a book beside me. The atmosphere was tense. Frustrated at how long the unpleasantness had lingered, I decided it was time to make peace. I turned toward my wife with loving intentions. I wanted to make a peace offering, but what started to come out of my mouth was a declaration of war.

I caught myself before I yelled, and shuddered silently at this grim realization: I still loved my wife, but I couldn't stop hating her. If we did not do something quickly, our marriage would either self-destruct or settle into an icy détente. Yet as long as we were still angry it would be impossible to act peaceably. "We have to talk," I said.

"There's nothing to talk about," she replied curtly.

"We don't have a choice," I insisted. "I'm scared. I can't stand hating you."

Instantly, my wife knew something had changed. I was talking *to* her, not *at* her. "I'm scared too," she confessed.

Our hands found each other under the blanket. It was the first time we had touched in weeks. Soon, we had the long, honest talk we so desperately needed.

From that point on, I have tried to help warring couples understand that it's futile to try to make up before letting go of the anger inside. Trying to be loving while still harboring hatred might buy you a truce, but not genuine peace. Hatred keeps you on guard. You get defensive over minor remarks and overreact to everything the other person does that's not totally, unequivocally positive. That's not exactly a recipe for intimacy. Only when you are drained of underlying negativity and come to feel punched out emotionally can you think, "I don't want to hate this person anymore." Then the rebuilding can begin on a solid foundation.

Hatred usually begins with disappointment. As you discover irritating qualities in your partner, you gradually come to think, "This is not the person I fell in love with." Initially, you hesitate to tell the other person because you don't want to hurt him. But if your feelings have no outlet, they build up, until you're afraid that if you admit how upset you are the relationship could not endure. In time, the disappointment turns to anger, and eventually the anger becomes chronic and turns into hatred.

Hating usually hurts the hater more than the one who is hated. I often ask couples, "If you had to choose between getting your way all the time and never having to feel angry toward your spouse, which would you take?" Nearly everyone says, "Never being angry again." Deep inside, most of us know that feeling hatred is much more painful than not getting our way. As one husband poignantly stated, "The only thing I hate more than my wife is hating her."

"You cannot shake hands with a clenched fist."
—INDIRA GANDHI

Can you imagine a worse fate than to come to the end of your life and realize that you hated well but loved poorly? If you'd like to thaw out the cold war between you and your partner, you have to get through the hate. Fortunately, while it might seem surprising, hatred is actually easier to overcome than the loss of love. When love really dies, it cannot be resurrected by an act of will. But if it has merely been obscured by a cloud of hate, it can shine again once the hate has dissipated.

USABLE INSIGHT:
Relationships end not because you stop loving, but because you can't stop hating each other.

TAKING ACTION

• Instead of being afraid to face your ugly feelings, give them a fantasy life in your mind. Imagine a hateful, vengeful action that matches your feeling and play it out mentally. Doing this can help you feel less out of control.

- Start talking to the other person from the hatred you feel on the surface, but don't stop until you get to the vulnerability that underlies the hostility. Emotions are built on layers. Beneath hatred is usually anger; beneath anger is frustration; beneath frustration is hurt; beneath hurt is fear. If you keep expressing your feelings, you will generally move through them in that order. What begins with "I hate you" culminates in "I'm scared. I don't want to lose you, and I don't know what to do about it."

- Once you've talked your way from hate to hurt and fear, you've laid the groundwork for a new beginning. To strengthen that foundation, try these exercises:
  - Both partners describe one of their own character flaws. Humility resolves self-righteousness.
  - Both partners share a quality of the other person that they admire. Admiration resolves disappointment.
  - Both partners express appreciation for something that the other one did. Gratitude resolves resentment.
  - Both partners apologize, without excuses, for something they did to hurt the other person. Remorse resolves hurt.

Both partners can now express what the other did or didn't do that hurt and angered them.

15

Not Learning From Your Mistakes

"Experience is the name everyone gives to
their mistakes."
—OSCAR WILDE

"If you don't learn from your mistakes, someone
else will."
—ANONYMOUS

Self-defeating behavior is inevitable when we don't learn the lessons that experience tries to teach us.

In an old sitcom episode, a character finds a pistol and decides to cash it in at a New York pawn shop. The clerk sees the gun and hits the alarm button. Complications follow, and in the end the character convinces the court he is innocent. Before letting him go, however, the judge says, "It is against the law to sell a gun in New York. What will you do if you find another one?"

"Pawn it in New Jersey," replies our hero.

That is an example of learning the wrong lesson from a mistake.

Perhaps the most common wrong lesson we derive from mistakes is to conclude that we should *avoid* similar situations in the future rather than learn how to handle them differently. While sometimes appropriate, "I won't try that again" or "I'll never go there again" is usually a way to spare yourself the pain of having to reconsider your actions. Taken to extremes, avoidance can even turn into a phobia, triggering anxiety every time you are in a situation that resembles the original trauma.

I once treated a young prosecuting attorney who was deeply depressed because she had blown her first trial. Eager to score a knockout, she worked extraordinarily long hours in preparation, depriving herself of sleep and sustenance. After pulling an all-nighter, she buzzed into the courtroom and delivered a brilliant opening statement, only to be stunned by the tactics of a wily defense attorney. Nervous and sleep-deprived, she lost her composure, stammering incoherently and fumbling in her briefcase for material she could not find. The judge declared a mistrial.

Sadly, the lesson she came away with was "I'm not cut out for criminal law." The right lessons would have been: keeping your mind and body sound is an important aspect of preparation; learn as much as you can about your opponent; and, one setback does not cancel out the skills that brought you this far.

Another common and unworthy reaction to a mistake is to judge yourself too harshly. Thoughts such as "I'm such a wimp!" "What an idiot!" or "I'm totally incompetent" can help you assuage feelings of guilt and shame by punishing yourself. They also enable you to beat others to the punch; if you criticize yourself strongly enough, nothing anyone else can say will possibly be as bad. In fact, when others sense your self-blame, they might back off from their own criticism and try to console you instead.

But self-flagellation is ultimately self-defeating. It's important to distinguish between *hating yourself* and *hating something you did.* "This proves I'm totally worthless" leads to despair and loss of confidence, while "I can't stand when I act that way" can lead to wisdom and determination.

Some wrong lessons are the same as denial. I have seen people who were caught having extramarital affairs conclude, after the bitter battles that followed, "I should have been more careful not to get caught." Such a self-centered reaction leads to cover-up behavior instead of growth. These people failed to learn the right lesson, namely to confront the relationship problems that drove them to have an affair.

Victims of abuse commonly take the opposite tack. I know battered wives who say, after each heartbreaking episode, "He didn't mean it. I should learn not to provoke him." Wrong lesson. What they need desperately to learn is: they don't deserve such treatment; they must stand up for themselves; they will not fall apart if they leave their husbands.

It is wrong to deny your mistakes and wrong not to learn from them. Those two wrongs cannot make things right, but facing your mistakes and learning the right lessons can.

USABLE INSIGHT:
We always learn from our mistakes, but we don't always learn the right lessons.

Taking Action

- When you make a mistake, don't let yourself make any irreversible decisions for at least 48 hours. Screwing up makes us feel as if something in the mind has fallen apart. In our rush to repair it, we grasp at an easy source of relief rather than evaluate our motives and actions. The 48-Hour Rule provides a grace period in which to figure out the right lesson.
- Ask yourself if you might be avoiding the *real* lesson because:

  - You'd rather have immediate gratification.
  - The truth is too hard to face.
  - It would require that you change.
  - You need to blame someone else.

- Allow yourself to hate the mistake you've made, but not to hate yourself.
- Think back to similar situations in the past. Did you make the same mistake then? If not, what did you do differently? If so, what did you tell yourself you would do if you had it to do over again? These memories might help you learn the right lesson.

16

Trying to Change Others

*"When we are no longer able to change a
situation, we are challenged to change ourselves."*
—VICTOR FRANKL

Recently I asked the four couples in a therapy group, "How many of you feel that if your relationship is to get better, your partner has to change?" Without hesitation, eight hands went up. Then I asked, "How many feel that *you* have to change?" After a moment of awkward hesitation, everyone raised a hand, not with conviction but because they knew it was expected of them.

Relationships often come to a standstill because both parties feel it is time for a change but each one thinks the other should do the changing. While they try to force the change, or wait for it to come about, they refuse to fully accept the other person. This is self-defeating because it usually provokes resistance, or even rebellion, not cooperation. Not only does no one change, but the relationship gets contaminated by resentment and bitterness. Perhaps the most common reason for divorce is that one partner fails to become the person the other dreamed of.

Rather than not accepting the other person until he changes, accept him as is and *hope* he changes.

Of course, certain attitudes and behaviors are un-acceptable and nonnegotiable. If that's what you're faced with, you have some serious thinking to do. Don't un-derestimate how difficult it can be—and how miserable you can become—if you try to change someone who has qualities you just cannot accept.

With anything short of that, however, the best strat-egy is to accept first and hope for change later. This does not necessarily mean you should keep quiet about your concerns. But it might mean conveying a more accepting attitude. A message such as "I love you, but this bothers me, and I hope very much that it can change" will gen-erate a more positive response than "You'd better change or else." Chances are, the traits you find objectionable bother the other person too; your acceptance might make him or her feel secure enough to work on improving.

Conditional acceptance is also a major issue between parents and children. Take, for example, Gail, a single mother, and her daughter Marcy. Gail wanted Marcy to grow up to be a self-sufficient woman, but Marcy seemed to have little ambition and even less discipline. In her zeal to instill the desired qualities in her daughter, Gail re-sorted to scolding and punishing. This would motivate Marcy for a while, but before long she would rebel again. She was willing to jeopardize her own future just to prove that she was her own person.

"Can you accept Marcy for just being herself?" I asked Gail. "If you can't, she's going to stay stuck, and you'll deprive yourself of the joy of being a mother."

It took a great deal of effort for Gail to accept her daughter as is, but the struggle paid off. Marcy actually *wanted* to behave differently, but she couldn't change unless she was certain it was her own choice, not just a way to win her mother's approval.

If you expect people to change, you can drive yourself crazy waiting for it to happen. If you try to make them change, you will drive *them* crazy. But if you accept them as they are and tell them that you hope they'll change, they just might do it.

USABLE INSIGHT:
Don't try to change people; accept them as they are and hope they'll change.

TAKING ACTION

- Next time you're frustrated with a person in your life, pause and ask yourself, "If he never changes, will that be okay? Will I be able to continue loving him anyway?" If the answer is yes, you should be able to change your expectations and still feel good about the relationship.
- Instead of feeling like a helpless victim, make an active, conscious choice to let him be who he is.
- List the person's good qualities and bad qualities.
- To truly accept him, spend some time developing an active appreciation of the good qualities.
- Choose to convert your *need* to change the bad qualities to the *hope* that he will change. *Your well-being should not depend on another person changing.*
- Take pride in knowing you have chosen to be gracious rather than bitter.

- If you choose to tell the person that you hope he changes, offer a tradeoff by asking, "Is there anything about me that you hope I change?" By leveling the playing field, you give him greater incentive to make the effort.

17

Rebelling Just for the Sake of Rebelling

*"The marvelous rebellion of man at all signs
reading 'Keep Off.' "*
—CARL SANDBURG

*"It's better to fight for something than
against something."*
—ANONYMOUS

Not long ago, at a psychiatric conference, I ran into someone I had known in college. I remembered Ted as a bright student who had gone on to graduate school to become a therapist like his mother and father. To my surprise, he turned out not to be a therapist at all but an administrator at a psychiatric hospital, and he was obviously self-conscious about it.

Ted dropped out of graduate school when he realized he had entered the field just to please his parents. He became a rebel with a cause—to be master of his own destiny. Unfortunately, he also became a rebel without a clue. He worked in a bookstore, tried unsuccessfully to launch a writing career, then opened a small bakery in a college town. For some years he was content to live a simple life doing his own thing. But, as he aged and started a family, discontentment grew like his waistline. Bored, and no longer satisfied to just scrape by, he called on family connections and obtained an administrative job in the mental health field.

Ted managed to build a respectable career, but now he felt unfulfilled. "I only get turned on when I'm with therapists, talking about real cases," he told me. "I keep up with the literature, and sometimes I have better ideas than the shrinks, but no one takes me seriously."

Clearly, Ted had regrets about his earlier decisions. "I might have missed my calling," he confessed. "I'd have been a damn good shrink."

Ted had rebelled against his parents, who had driven him to become a therapist. Internally, he shouted, "Don't tell me what to do!" and in the process he'd muffled his own voice.

Children who are pushed to lead a certain kind of life often get confused: "Am I doing this for myself or for my parents? Is this what I really want, or am I just going along with their game plan?" With their free will threatened, doing what is right for them becomes less important than asserting their independence. And the outcome of their choices becomes less important than making sure the choices are their own. Sometimes that independent spirit pays off in a more authentic life. But when what's expected of them happens to be in sync with who they are and what they want, they can end up rebelling against themselves.

This form of self-defeating behavior is not limited to children rebelling against parents. I've seen countless husbands and wives who were in constant rebellion against spouses they perceived to be bossy. I've seen business partners, especially siblings in family-owned companies, rebel against each other's demands to the detriment of the bottom line. Invariably, the problem is not that the rebel doesn't *want* to do what's being asked, it's that he or she doesn't want to *have* to do it. Being forced or coerced destroys our self-respect and compromises our dignity. It makes us feel like children.

The key is to be able to feel that you are choosing your actions, not merely going along to satisfy someone else. When you find yourself rejecting the wishes of others, make sure you are not rejecting your own as well. One clue is whether you have a clear and desirable alternative in mind. If, for example, Ted had had a genuine passion for writing, or dreamed of owning a bakery, it might not have been a mistake to drop out of graduate school.

As for dealing with a demanding spouse or colleague, instead of rebelling reflexively or grudgingly going along, pause and ask yourself if the request is fair and reasonable. If it is, then *choose* to do it. If it's not, either say no or do it as a favor and let the person know that you expect something in return. When the time is right, explain that you can't choose to do something of your own free will if you are being ordered to do it. As one of my patients told her husband, "I'm an adult, and I don't want to do things out of fear or intimidation."

Sometimes it is noble, and even courageous, to rebel, but the satisfaction will be short-lived if, in the name of standing up for yourself, you sabotage yourself instead.

USABLE INSIGHT:
You won't resent having to do something if you
choose to do it.

TAKING ACTION

- When others put pressure on you, pause and ask yourself if they are being fair and reasonable.
- Analyze objectively whether it makes sense for you to do what they're urging you to do.
- Ask yourself, "If they were to change their opinions, or disappear tomorrow, would I follow their original wishes?" You might draw a blank at first, but if you keep thinking in those terms your deepest desires will eventually emerge.
- If your own aspirations turn out to be consistent with their expectations, shift your mind-set so that you actively *choose* that alternative. In this way, you assert that no one else controls you, and you keep your self-esteem.

18

Talking When Nobody's Listening

"Talking is like playing on the harp; there is as much in laying the hands on the strings to stop their vibration as in twanging them to bring out their music."
—*OLIVER WENDELL HOLMES*

I attended a seminar once where the contrast between two of the speakers made a lasting impression. Dr. Bernhardt was a charismatic entertainer. He knew how to engage an audience and generate enthusiasm. Dr. Smith was quiet and thoughtful, but not terribly inspiring. At first, the participants raved about the magnetic Bernhardt and joked about the boring Smith, but ultimately it was the latter who won over the group. She had been mindful of her audience. She had taken their questions seriously and listened to their concerns. Dr. Bernhardt had used them only as a foil for his routine.

Perhaps the most notable distinction between the speakers was this: Bernhardt exceeded his time limit at every session and seemed to resent it when people started to fidget. Dr. Smith was more tuned in. At the first sign of restlessness, she would suggest taking a break. She never wore out her welcome.

Why do we keep talking when people have heard enough? When we badly need to be heard, our conversation usually proceeds in three distinct phases. The first is an effort to communicate information or express a point of view. Once that is accomplished, other needs take over. In the second stage, the principal motivation is to relieve tension. Gabbing away just to make ourselves feel better, we repeat or rephrase what we have already said, or introduce irrelevant subjects. In the third phase we detour into any area that might keep the listener's attention, just to keep from being abandoned. In sum, the motivation shifts from the need to communicate, to the need to relieve tension, to the need to retain control.

The listener who gets dragged into phases two and three is placed in the difficult position of having to find a way out without being impolite. If she can't, she ends up wasting her time and becoming exasperated. For the overzealous speaker, the price is even higher; she stands to lose respect, and possibly even friends.

In times of stress or excitement the tension from keeping our feelings and thoughts to ourselves builds up. To many of us, it feels so good to unload that we forget our manners. We go from dialogue to monologue, launching an avalanche of words, unable to stop ourselves before becoming tiresome or rude.

> *"Blessed is the man who, having nothing to say,*
> *abstains from giving in words evidence*
> *of the fact."*
> —GEORGE ELIOT

If you have this tendency, try to be aware of the stages of conversation and apply the brakes before you enter the annoying second stage or the impertinent third stage. Keep an eye on the other person's body language. If she fidgets or glances at her watch, or her eyes become less focused, she is probably trying to figure out a way to cut you off without being discourteous. Your initial impulse might be to hold her attention by any means possible. But it's self-defeating to hold someone's attention by holding her hostage.

You have to decide if the relief you will get from continuing is worth the price. What is the price? The other person will probably tune you out or make up an excuse to interrupt you. You can end up feeling embarrassed, foolish or worse. If you wear out your welcome often enough, you'll find that people ignore you, "forget" to return your phone calls and exclude you from gatherings.

Unless your need for immediate gratification is stronger than your need for friends, learn to control yourself. Remember, you will be appreciated and admired if you don't pressure others to keep listening when they've heard enough. But if you use them as tension relievers (phase two) and try to dominate their attention (phase three), you might hold on to them for the moment but lose them for the future.

USABLE INSIGHT:
When people stop listening, stop talking.

TAKING ACTION

- If you want to know if you're talking too long, keep your eye on the other person's body language.

- If you notice signs of restlessness, ask yourself which you would rather feel: the frustration of not completing what you've started to say, or the humiliation of talking when no one's listening.
- Stop yourself as soon as possible.
- Solicit the other person's ideas and comments. By turning your monologue into a dialogue, you might extend your welcome instead of wearing it out.

19

Pretending You're Fine
When You're Not

"Dare to be true: nothing can need a lie: A fault,
which needs it most, grows two thereby."
—*GEORGE HERBERT*

John, a 43-year-old hardware store manager, was telling me about an upcoming visit from his parents, who lived out of town. I asked if he was looking forward to seeing them.

"It'll be fine," he said.

"You don't sound very convincing," I replied.

"Well, they bicker constantly, and criticize everything I do. But they're in their late seventies, so I guess I'm lucky they're still alive."

I pushed John to express what he really felt. He admitted that he couldn't stand his parents' visits. "It drains me," he said. "Nobody enjoys it, not even them."

John's typical response was to withdraw into a sullen, pouty silence. His parents would ask, "Is something wrong?" and he would say, "No, no, I'm fine." In most instances he couldn't even admit to himself that something was wrong.

This sort of denial is common. Admitting to yourself that you are upset or in pain can make you feel exposed. You fear that acknowledging a bad feeling gives it more power. The pain might get worse. You might not be able to tolerate it. In fact, the opposite is usually true: recognizing a feeling releases pent-up tension and makes you feel better rather than worse.

You might also fear that you won't be able to say, "I feel bad" without blaming someone. Then you'll have to either retaliate or, if you blame yourself, feel ashamed. You might even be forced to take action, and that prospect can be frightening: "What if I don't have the skill or wisdom to make things better?" you wonder. "What if I have to do something risky?" It's a lot easier to exempt yourself by not admitting you feel bad in the first place.

As I told John, it's important to realize that *being* okay doesn't mean *feeling* okay all the time. Rather, it means being able to experience appropriate feelings without denial, self-deception or repression. Mentally healthy people feel what they are supposed to feel: when they are angry, they feel anger; when they are sad, they feel sadness. Owning up to the feeling is the first necessary step toward feeling better.

It is also important to realize that acknowledging bad feelings doesn't mean you have to do anything about them. In fact, telling yourself you feel bad actually diminishes the need to act. It stifles the impulse to take sudden, precipitous action, which could make things worse.

I suggested to John that when his parents started to get to him, he should say to himself, "I hate the way I feel." He seemed puzzled but agreed to try it. The next time I saw him he said, "As soon as I told myself 'I hate the way I feel,' I felt relieved." He was able to tolerate his parents without pouting or withdrawing—and without blowing up when they continued to annoy him.

Admitting to yourself that you feel bad is, of course, a prerequisite to admitting it to others. In an effort to conceal your troubles, you might avoid, or lie to, the very people who can help you. Covering up not only keeps you from getting help, it creates a vicious cycle: it makes you become agitated and defensive; the people around you get irritated; then you feel worse because you can't understand how anyone could be upset with you when you feel so bad.

Admitting that you're not okay requires a leap of faith. You have to believe that the temporary discomfort of owning up to the feeling is better than the long-term consequences of repression and avoidance. That faith can give you the courage to hang in there until you can actually make things better.

USABLE INSIGHT:
You have to admit that you feel bad before you can feel better.

TAKING ACTION

• The next time you feel bad, acknowledge the upset inwardly. This simple act is calming and helps prevent a hasty reaction.
• Give the feeling a name. This makes it less threat-

ening and more manageable. If you can name it you can tame it.

- Name it as accurately as possible. "I'm upset" is okay for a start, but something like "I feel discouraged" or "I feel hopeless" is probably more precise.
- If you decide to let someone else know you feel bad, indicate exactly *how* bad. You can do this by saying, "It feels so bad it makes me want to _____." Such examples show rather than tell about feelings, making them more understandable to others. Others will listen better and will probably offer the empathy you deserve.

20

Becoming Obsessive or Compulsive

*"I was seized by the stern hand of Compulsion,
that dark, unseasonable Urge that impels women
to clean house in the middle of the night."*
—JAMES THURBER

*"Just because you need to doesn't mean you
have to."*
—ANONYMOUS

Sometimes, when we are pressured, we can feel pushed to the edge, as if we might lose control at any moment. To avert disaster, the mind redirects our attention. We focus on things that appear to be controllable. When taken too far, this defense can lead to obsessions and compulsions. Ironically, these develop a life of their own, leaving us to feel even more powerless.

An obsession is an unconscious attempt to turn an overwhelming feeling into a thought. You replay the thought pattern over and over to divert your mind until the discomfort passes. But the effect is much like treading water: you waste a lot of energy and end up getting nowhere.

Obsessions invariably grow stronger with time. When they reach a certain magnitude, the mental energy overflows from thought into behavior. The result is what we call a compulsion. For example, a child gets lost in a department store. The terror of being suddenly alone and unprotected is so unbearable that he fixates on his scuffed shoes in an attempt to hold off the fear until Mommy returns. If the obsession builds to where the child has to act on it, he begins compulsively wiping his shoes.

Most of us are familiar with the many adult versions of this pattern: someone who feels like a failure obsesses about getting rich quick, and that leads to compulsive gambling; someone who feels ugly obsesses about the appearance of her home and then compulsively decorates; someone who feels empty inside obsesses about how to fill herself up and becomes a compulsive eater.

The key to breaking the obsession or compulsion is to confront head-on the pain or fear that gave rise to it. As a rule, the longer you avoid the root issues, the more powerless you feel and the more consuming the obsession and compulsion become. The best approach is to retrace the process in reverse. First, stop the compulsive behavior, whether it is washing your hands, cleaning your house, having sex with dangerous partners or whatever. This might not be easy; it can create anxiety similar to that of an addict going through withdrawal, since a compulsion is, in a sense, an addiction to a dysfunctional way of coping.

When you cease the compulsive behavior, your system will back up to what preceded it: obsessive thinking. Since it no longer has an outlet in behavior, the obsession will escalate. Eventually it will build to a point where you are forced to pay attention to the core feelings that set the pattern in motion in the first place. If you have the courage to let the process run its course, you might come to see clearly the pain or fear you have been avoiding.

Let's look at two examples from my practice. Joe, an engineer in the aerospace industry, became obsessed with his computer files. He thought they were in danger of being destroyed by a virus. He compulsively applied antivirus programs and created elaborate systems to protect his files. It reached the point where he was spending more time safeguarding his computer than doing his job. At my urging, he promised to stop his campaign the next morning. He did, but he could not stop thinking about the threat of a virus, and left work to see me. I helped him discover his real fear. His industry had been beset by layoffs, and he was afraid of losing his job. Beneath that, he was terrified of repeating the fate of his father, who had to be committed to a state mental hospital after getting fired from a long-held job. Now able to see his real fears and anxieties, he was able to take proactive steps to increase his worth to his company rather than continuing his useless obsessions and compulsions.

Irene was a single mother who worked long hours to support her children. On weekends she would compensate by compulsively organizing family activities. Now the kids were rebelling against the pressure she put on them to enjoy themselves all the time. I convinced Irene to plan nothing for the following weekend. As Friday approached, she became more and more anxious, until she finally came face to face with her core issue: she feared that she was, like her own mother, incapable of genuine emotional involvement with those she loved. Admitting and facing her fears of not being emotionally caring enabled her to take steps to indulge her children less and involve herself with them more.

Breaking free of an obsession and its accompanying compulsion is not easy, particularly if the pattern has become entrenched. But you can and must do it if you are going to run your life rather than run from it.

USABLE INSIGHT:
Obsessions and compulsions can help you get past
pain and fear, but they won't help you get
over them.

TAKING ACTION

- Identify your obsessions by listing all the thoughts you dwell on continuously that don't lead to constructive action.
- Identify your compulsions by listing repetitive behaviors that give you relief at the moment but make you feel guilty afterward or create additional problems.
- Promise yourself that next time you are about to launch into these thoughts or behaviors, you will stop yourself.
- If terminating the compulsive behavior is too difficult to handle alone, enlist the support of a therapist, pastor or friend. A trusted person who will stand by you can be indispensable in this phase.
- If you find yourself slipping into an unwanted action, say to yourself, "Oh, I forgot. I don't do this any-

more." It's a simple reminder that you have made a commitment to no longer engage in that self-destructive behavior.

- When you stop the compulsive behavior, tension will increase. Become aware of the physical and emotional sensations. Ask, "What do I feel and where do I feel it?"

- After you identify the sensations, complete the following sentences: "When I feel this way, it makes me want to _____." "If I do that, the consequences will be _____." "A better thing to do now would be _____."

- Reward yourself each time you don't give in to an obsession or compulsion. Eventually, feeling that you're no longer in the grip of obsessions and compulsions will be reward enough.

Note: The obsessive and compulsive behavior discussed here should not be confused with obsessive-compulsive disorder, a serious psychiatric condition that often requires medication.

21

Taking Things Too Personally

*"It's not a slam at you when people are rude—
it's a slam at the people they've met before."*
—F. SCOTT FITZGERALD

"At ev'ry trifle scorn to take offense."
—ALEXANDER POPE

*"There are offences given and offences not given
but taken."*
—IZAAK WALTON

"I told you kids to shut up!" With that, Maureen, a 43-year-old labor relations attorney, jerked her arm toward the backseat to grab the nearest wrist. The car swerved into the adjacent lane of the freeway, coming within inches of smashing into an oncoming truck. The close call got the kids to stop screaming all right, but it also nearly killed them.

Maureen was so upset by the incident that she unleashed a torrent of self-hatred in my office. "Look at me," she cried. "Ms. Super Lawyer who stands up to labor unions but can't control her own kids without murdering them." I asked what she does when opposing lawyers attack her. "I try not to take it personally," she said. "If I let it get to me, I couldn't think clearly."

It was a perfect response. Maureen realized that she had reacted in the car as if the children were misbehaving just to aggravate her. She had taken it as a personal affront, whereas they were merely releasing pent-up energy after sitting in a classroom all day. I suggested that if it were to happen again she should take it seriously, but not personally.

Taking something personally means assuming that a particular remark or action was intended to hurt you. You might, for example, take a well-meant correction as a criticism, or a disagreement as a put-down, or an innocent comment about a third party as an insult aimed at you. For example, when the wife of a struggling author mentioned a first-time novelist who had signed a huge contract, her husband was outraged. He felt that his wife was really saying, "You're a failure." In reality, she felt that someone with her husband's talent deserved the same kind of break.

Failing to consider the other person's true intention is a good way to ruin a relationship. Instead of reflecting and responding appropriately, you merely react, either retaliating or becoming defensive, sullen or petulant. Such responses not only obscure the legitimate reasons for your concern but poison the other person's response to your legitimate grievances. And, when you realize what you've done, you end up feeling ashamed in the bargain.

Taking things personally can also be bad for business. Take the case of Joanna, the founder and owner of a medical supply company. At an important meeting, while she prepped her sales force on a new line of products, a salesman named Tim yawned conspicuously. To Joanna, who had hired Tim and considered him a protégé, the yawn felt like a slap in the face, a public display of disrespect. She fired him on the spot. Tim hit back with a wrongful termination suit. It was not until the damage was done that Joanna realized that Tim had been one of the company's hardest-working salesmen. He'd been working long hours, and his yawn had more to do with exhaustion than disrespect. To her credit, Joanna apologized for her error and rehired Tim.

Taking things personally can make you hot under the collar, or it can turn you cold. A surprising number of men have told me that they separated from their wives because they were so angry over repeated affronts that they were afraid they might become violent. Others are so horrified by their anger that they simply turn off, withdrawing affection and attention from the very person they want most to give it to. Tragically, in many of those cases, the pain is caused by actions that should never have been taken personally. When you learn to take things seriously instead, you not only cool off, you can once again warm up to those you had been angry at.

USABLE INSIGHT:
Don't take it personally, take it seriously.

TAKING ACTION

- When someone does something to upset you, ask yourself if you did anything to justify his or her action.

- If you did, it is better to own up to it early. Offer an apology and promise to try to do better next time.
- If you didn't do anything to justify the behavior, ask yourself if the other person is this way with others too. If so, don't take it personally.
- You have three choices: find a way to be more accepting; cut your losses and end the relationship; make your feelings known and hope the offensive behavior stops.
- Remember, not taking things personally does not mean turning the other cheek. It means shooting from the head rather than the hip.

22

Acting Too Needy

"All men have need of the gods."
—HOMER

Everyone needs other people. But need becomes self-defeating when it is relentless, insatiable and presented in such a way as to make others feel put upon.

If you come across as needy, others see you as grabbing. They feel either that you are trying to get more than you are entitled to or more than you can give in return. The problem isn't asking for too much by way of tangible favors or material assistance, although that may be part of it. What upsets people is *emotional* neediness.

"Who depends on another man's table
often dines late."
—JOHN RAY

If neediness is your basic modus operandi, you look to others to validate you, reassure you and reinforce your worth. This is more than most people are capable of giving. Unless they are saints for whom virtue is its own reward, they will sooner or later turn away, when something they once gave freely comes to feel like an obligation. Feelings of resentment arise, and they start to dread being in contact with you.

Some of the neediest people act precisely the opposite way. They try to keep their neediness under control and out of awareness by coming across as *unneedy*. The prideful ones act as if they need nothing. We tend to see them as arrogant or condescending. We also find them exasperating because they make us feel unnecessary and perhaps ashamed for needing anything ourselves. It is difficult to have a relationship with such unneedy people because they deny us the opportunity to give, and most of us measure our worth at least in part by our ability to give something of value to others.

Another way to come across as unneedy is to act like a martyr. False martyrs are infuriating, because if you give to them they make you feel wrong for doing so. Then, just when they've convinced you that they don't need anything, they spring a major demand. If you fail to comply, they act hurt and remind you of all they have done for you. And if you try to make up for it, they say, "Don't do me any favors." People eventually get tired of the mixed messages and stop trying to figure out what the martyr actually needs.

Neediness usually results when childhood insecurity turns into the adult fear of not being able to stand on one's own two feet. Other people come to be seen as rescuers. The challenge is to accept insecurities and fears as something everyone has to deal with and move on.

In many cases, though, the problem isn't being needy but *acting* needy. Some of us come across as a lot more dependent than we actually are. If you find yourself doing that, try instead to present yourself as what I call *needful.* Needful people demonstrate an acceptable level of need. Others help them willingly because they ask for what is reasonable, and when they get it they show appreciation and a willingness to reciprocate. If they can't get what they need, they manage to make do and not hold it against you.

The needful make requests; the needy make demands. The needful depend on others; the needy are dependent. The needful are genuinely grateful; the needy use gratitude as a way to hook others into the next round of giving. If you act needy, people will see you as a taker—and it is very hard to give to a taker. But if you act needful, people will see you as reaching out for what you deserve rather than grabbing. In all likelihood, they will give you what you need.

USABLE INSIGHT:
Being needy begets resentment. Being unneedy begets frustration. Being needful begets help.

TAKING ACTION

- Realize that if you're too demanding, people may initially give you what you want, but they'll soon start to resent you.
- Realize that if you act *unneedy*, you make it impossible for people to give to you, and they will feel frustrated.
- Learn to express clearly what you need from others, and don't make it sound like a demand.

- Make sure others know you are willing to reciprocate and that it's okay for them to need you.
- When you get what you need, show genuine appreciation.
- Be prepared to take no for an answer without getting upset or holding a grudge.

23

Having Unrealistic Expectations

"Oft expectation fails, and most oft there
Where most it promises."
—SHAKESPEARE

Maxine came to me for help with what seemed to be a reasonable goal: to get back together with her ex-husband. She mentioned several perfectly good reasons why the marriage would work like a dream this time around, even though the first attempt had been a nightmare. She knew what had gone wrong and exactly what she and her ex-husband had to do to fix the relationship. Having personally helped many ex-spouses to recouple, I thought she was approaching the reconciliation sensibly. It was only when I asked about her ex-husband's attitude that I realized how deluded she was. Her former spouse had already remarried and fathered two children.

Maxine had turned something she wanted into something she absolutely had to have, and then held onto that attitude even after her goal had turned into a pipe dream. She not only set herself up to be devastated, she allowed her fantasy to consume time and energy that might have been used to improve her life or develop a *real* relationship.

In my experience, most of our expectations are fair and reasonable. However, they are not always realistic. It is reasonable to start a new career at midlife, but it is not realistic to expect it to be easy or result in immediate success. It is reasonable to expect a friend to understand your feelings, but it might not be realistic if he or she is a very analytic, solution-oriented person.

People who habitually choose unrealistic goals allow wishful thinking to override their grip on common sense. In their minds, if they want something, it must be feasible to attain it. They like to gamble on big payoffs, but they need a Las Vegas bookmaker to help them calculate the odds. They don't assess realistically whether they have the talent, resources and savvy to realize their dreams, and whether conditions are favorable. To make matters worse, they are usually so sure of their prospects that they fail to set up contingency plans or prepare themselves emotionally for defeat. As a result, they don't merely have setbacks, they fall back all the way to square one, and sometimes even further. And each loss increases the need for quick vindication, which makes longshots even more attractive.

> *"Attachment is the great fabricator of illusions;*
> *reality can be attained only by someone*
> *who is detached."*
> —SIMONE WEIL

Of course, it's fine to be a big thinker if you're also a big doer. Real doers and visionaries are different from unrealistic dreamers in these respects: they take pleasure in the sheer pursuit of their goals, not just the outcome;

they know that if they fall on their faces they can pick themselves up and be okay; they know the odds and are prepared for possible defeat. One hugely successful entrepreneur I know has turned many a long shot into a victory. He takes on risky projects all the time, but he has no illusions about their potential and prepares himself financially and emotionally to not be devastated if he should fail.

If you are going to take on long shots, it is not only vital to have the wherewithal to achieve them but to make sure you can handle failure. If you *want* to have something and you don't get it, you'll be disappointed. If you *need* to have it and you don't get it, you'll be depressed. If you *just gotta* have it and you don't get it, you'll be devastated.

I encourage my patients to appraise how realistic their goals are and to set their expectations appropriately. If your goal is unrealistic, don't go after it with a "gotta have it" attitude. It's far safer to lean toward needing it or wanting it. This is especially true in relationships. As a rule, since other people are so unpredictable, it is best to treat your expectations as wants.

If you treat a long shot like a sure thing, it's a sure thing you will end up disappointed. But if you treat a long shot like a long shot and a sure thing like a sure thing, you are a good bet to get everything you deserve out of life.

USABLE INSIGHT:
Just because it's reasonable doesn't mean it's
realistic.

Taking Action

- Next time you want something, ask yourself how likely it is to happen.
- List everything that's necessary to achieve your goal.
- Look at yourself objectively and evaluate your ability to accomplish what has to be done.
- Rate your goal on a scale of 1–10 with 1 being totally unrealistic and 10 being a sure thing. The lower the score, the more important it is to have a backup plan that will work.
- Set your expectation level at "want to have it," "need to have it," or "gotta have it," according to how realistic your goal is.
- Try not to feel "gotta have it" with a long shot unless you're prepared to be devastated.

24

Trying to Take Care of Everybody

"It is easier to mend neglect than
to quicken love."
—SAINT JEROME

"I don't know the key to success, but the key to
failure is to try to please everyone."
—BILL COSBY

Whenever I feel overextended, I think of the street performer in Venice, California, who juggles chain saws. I am awed by the intensity with which he concentrates on each ferocious saw as he plucks it from the air. The slightest distraction, and he could easily lose an arm.

Like the juggler, I need to focus sharply on each role I play—husband, father, son, brother, therapist, friend, teacher—only in some respects my task is harder: the performer juggles chain saws, but I have to juggle people. Because all my roles are important, and the amount of time I can give to them is limited, I have to make sure that every person who matters to me does not feel neglected.

For a busy person, trying to do justice to everyone's needs is self-defeating because you usually end up doing justice to no one, including yourself. If you spread yourself too thin, you not only risk burnout but the scorn and anger of people who expect you to be there for them.

> *"The fact is that the Americans are not a*
> *thoughtful people; they are too busy to stop and*
> *question their values."*
> —*WILLIAM RALPH*

The key is to make each person *feel* important when you're with them. Of the many busy people I know, the ones who manage their juggling acts best are those who give each activity and each person their undivided attention. At the office, they are totally engaged in their work; at home, the office is history and they focus on their roles as spouses and parents; when they are with their mother, boss or accountant, they are immersed in the roles of adult child, employee or client. Each entrance and exit is crisp, and most of the time no one feels shortchanged.

I say "most of the time" because there are always periods in a busy person's life when loved ones *do* feel shortchanged. When that happens, I advise the person to tell others, "You're the most important spouse I have. You kids are the most important children I have. My career is the most important career I have. And I'm the most important self I have. If I've made you feel unappreciated, then I've been remiss. I'm sorry, but please understand that every part of my life is important."

However, you have to do more than explain. You can demonstrate someone's importance only through your actions. If, for example, you fail to deliver on your promises, no amount of comforting words will make your child or spouse feel valued. It is also important to be proactive rather than reactive. People feel important not when you comply with their requests but when you initiate commitments on your own. Agreeing to show up at your kid's soccer game is one thing, but it is quite another to say, without being reminded, "You have a big game coming up, don't you? I can't wait to see it."

If you make people feel important, they won't feel deprived of your time. But keep the following caveats in mind. First, beware of doling out your time so equitably that *everyone* feels deprived. Some people *are* more important than others; make sure they know it. Second, you too are important, so don't feel guilty about devoting time to yourself. Third, as long as everyone is making a sincere effort to be fair, you and the people in your life should cut each other some slack. The way society is structured, the amount of time we spend on something often bears no relation to the true value we assign to it.

Juggling people may not be as physically dangerous as juggling chain saws, but it does entail risks. If you get careless, you won't sever an arm, but you might sever a valued relationship. If you make people feel important, however, you can hold onto everyone without fear of losing your grip.

USABLE INSIGHT:
Everything competes for time, but no one should have to compete for importance.

TAKING ACTION

One way to show people how much you value them is to demonstrate the Three C's:

- *Concern.* Let them express worries, fears and frustrations without interrupting or rushing them.
- *Curiosity.* Show an interest in them before they ask you to. "Did you have a good day?" does not convey much interest, whereas "How did that meeting go?" shows that you are aware of, and care about, the details of their lives.
- *Confidence.* Show respect for them and faith in their ability to handle problems. Instead of leaping in with advice, ask questions such as "What do you think you'll do next?" or "When will you let them know your decision?"

25

Refusing to "Play Games"

"When the One Great Scorer comes to write
against your name—
He marks—not that you won or lost—but how
you played the game."
—GRANTLAND RICE

"In play there are two pleasures for your
choosing—
The one is winning, and the other losing."
—LORD BYRON

People often complain to me about the game-playing of lovers, family members and business associates. Sometimes they refuse to play the game because they have legitimate moral objections or feel irate over having been manipulated. However, in most cases they bow out for less compelling reasons and deny themselves the rewards of the game. They lie to themselves that they're "above" the game or that the goal of the game is unimportant to them. What they're really concerned about is their inability to play the game as well as they would like.

Show me someone who says, "I can't stand playing games," and in most cases I'll show you someone who plays them poorly. A good example was a salesperson in the chemical industry named Beth. Competent and exceptionally driven, she had never quite achieved the level of success to which she had aspired. Of her peers who *had* reached those heights, she would scoff, "They're game-players. They schmooze, they flatter, they go to the right parties. I can't stand all that phoniness, otherwise I'd be where they are."

Beth pretended she was above it all when in fact she was simply out of it. A trained chemist, she had entered sales because of the earning potential but found that her scientific expertise was not enough. She was socially awkward. People felt uncomfortable around her. But, rather than acquire the social skills that grease the wheels of commerce, she adopted an air of self-righteousness that only alienated people further.

> *"Life is the game that must be played."*
> —*EDWIN ARLINGTON ROBINSON*

Some games are clearly not worth playing. These include games in which the intent is to harm others; games that demand that players be deceptive, devious, or cutthroat; and games whose penalty for losing is excessive. Playing such games will usually damage your self-respect or your reputation. You not only lose friends and influence no one, but you can also become paranoid; inside, you think that if you're being devious, others are probably doing the same to you. And your guilty conscience will one day demand penance.

However, many games are not only harmless, but valuable and life-enhancing; rather than being cold and ruthless, they are actually expressions of sensitivity. Perhaps the best example I've ever heard was the game played between Iris and Henry McCarver throughout their 55-year marriage. When Henry was dying, confined to a hospital bed with a morphine drip to dull his pain, Iris was at his side constantly. At one point she touched her husband tenderly on the back of his hand. "I have a confession to make," she whispered. "All these years I've been absolutely crazy about you. I always wanted you, but I played hard to get because I knew how much you liked the chase."

Summoning his strength, Henry smiled and said, "That's one of the things I loved you for."

Even those who advocate honesty at any cost would have to see the beauty of their little game.

Ultimately, what counts is not whether you win or lose but whether the game is worth playing. Games that unfairly take advantage of others are likely to confirm the adage, "What goes around comes around." Worthwhile games exploit opportunities rather than people, have clear and fair rules, and are not zero-sum—that is, no one has to lose in order for someone to win.

USABLE INSIGHT:
The best defense against game-playing is to play the game well.

TAKING ACTION

- When you find yourself reluctant to play a game, determine if it's because you don't want to or because you don't know how to.

- If you don't want to play, ask yourself why. If the answer is satisfactory, don't play.
- If you decide to play, find out what you have to do to play the game well. One way is to study what a winning player does.
- Learn the rules. In both interpersonal and institutional games, the rules are often unexpressed. Half the battle is figuring them out.
- Know your capacities. Do you have what it takes to play the game well?
- Know the other players. Who are your adversaries? Who are your allies? Whom can you trust?
- Learn to keep your cool. Many games are lost because a player tightens up when faced with the unexpected. Use the art of the timely pause to keep your wits about you.
- Know your limits. Are there aspects of game-playing that would compromise your dignity to the extent that you would have to stop playing?

26

Putting on an Act to Make a Good Impression

"This above all: to thine own self be true,
and it must follow, as the night the day,
thou canst not then be false to any man."
—SHAKESPEARE

"Looks like I'm headed for another love-hate relationship," said Carol. "You know, the kind where I love him and hate me."

To her credit, Carol still had a sense of humor, even after a series of disastrous relationships. Raised to be modest and to defer to others, she had married a controlling, self-absorbed man, divorced him, then found herself dating other men exactly like him. "Their interest in me extended to how much interest I showed in them," she said. Now 34 and a successful photographer, she was determined to find a man who would return the concern she was accustomed to giving.

She had recently met a man she liked, but on their first date she found herself slipping into the same pattern. Paul spoke mainly about himself and made all the decisions about what they would do, and Carol held back;

she did not talk about her work or express her opinions, and she deferred to all of Paul's suggestions.

"We are betrayed by what is false within."
—*GEORGE MEREDITH*

Like Carol, we all try to put our best foot forward at the beginning of a relationship. Because we want to be accepted, we mind our manners, try not to offend and conceal our flaws and weaknesses. Men usually try to convey an impression of competence while keeping a lid on how needy or possessive they can be. They might try to portray themselves as sensitive, but few will actually *show* their vulnerability; to do so would be to admit they can be hurt, and in their eyes that is equivalent to being weak. Women, on the other hand, tend to downplay their strength and accomplishments so as not to intimidate men. They are also leery of coming across as demanding or insecure, knowing that those qualities can push a man away. So, like Carol, they make a great effort to be attentive and agreeable.

However, there comes a time in every relationship when the parties let their guards down. Hidden flaws, needs and imperfections begin to leak out, and the longer they have been concealed, the stronger the shock and the greater the disruption to the relationship.

The problem is often made worse by another form of not being real: allowing someone's insensitive or hurtful behavior to pass without comment. We fear that if we try to hold the other person accountable, we will seem demanding and drive him or her away. Unfortunately, if we fail to express disapproval, the unacceptable traits can become habitual. Our resentment builds, and we eventually end up overreacting. Then we seem more than demanding; we seem abrasive and intolerant.

As I told Carol, it is crucial to put your *real* foot forward as early in the relationship as possible. Otherwise, the other person will grow to like someone you are not, and that leads only to trouble. Intimacy is built on trust. If you don't trust the other person enough to be yourself, you can't be intimate, and neither can he or she. Also, someone who lives a lie usually comes across as weak. In Carol's case, the men she worked so hard to please would invariably lose respect for her—and so would she.

"Right now, Paul likes how you make him feel," I told her. "But *you'll* feel better if he likes you for who you really are." I urged her to find a way to show Paul she was not some self-sacrificing woman who would tolerate a self-centered man. If he couldn't handle it, he was the wrong guy for her.

> *"The highest compact we can make with our*
> *fellow is—'Let there be truth between us two*
> *forevermore.' "*
> —*RALPH WALDO EMERSON*

What Carol did was so creative it won my lasting admiration. Over dinner on their next date, as Paul was rambling on about his business, she looked at him with an enigmatic smile. Intrigued, he asked, "What are you thinking?"

"I was just trying to figure out if you were a jerk,"

said Carol. "If you *are*, we can still be friends. I just want to be clear from the start."

Paul was secure enough to laugh. "I guess I can be awfully full of myself when I'm trying to impress someone," he said.

"That's okay," said Carol playfully. "I can be a real bitch myself."

Carol's unusual approach demonstrated that she was a confident woman who did not suffer fools gladly. It commanded Paul's interest, not to mention his respect. His next words were, "Well, that's a start. I want to know everything about you." Her honesty also had the salutary effect of encouraging Paul to relax and put *his* real foot forward.

> *"Truth is such a rare thing, it is delightful*
> *to tell it."*
> —EMILY DICKINSON

The next time you find yourself putting up a false front, ask yourself why you would want to be around someone who likes what you're not. But before you display yourself in all your truthful splendor, understand that if you reveal too much too soon, you can scare the other person away. One patient of mine would pour forth virtually her entire biography the minute she met an attractive man, along with a checklist of exactly what she was looking for in a relationship. The men felt like they were at an audition, not on a date. On the other hand, if you wait too long, tension will accumulate, and when the charade finally ends, the other person will probably feel resentful. Mark Twain was surely right when he said,

"When in doubt tell the truth." But I'm sure he would agree that in truth-telling, as in comedy, timing is everything.

USABLE INSIGHT:
Put your real foot forward first.

TAKING ACTION

- Be yourself from the very beginning of a relationship. Why would you want to be involved with someone who doesn't like you for you?
- Be honest without being blunt. Express your needs, wishes or frustrations as statements of your feelings, not as demands or ultimatums. For instance, "It frustrates me when you say we need to talk and then interrupt me if I say something you don't like."
- When sharing your troubles, don't make the other person feel sorry for you or responsible for solving your problems.
- When you talk about things you're proud of, do so without arrogance or conceit.
- When you express disapproval about someone's behavior, a) preface it by saying something positive about him, b) use nonjudgmental phrases such as, "It upsets me when . . ." and c) invite him to share something about you that upsets him.
- Once you've put your real foot forward, keep it there. It usually takes real perseverance to get into the habit of being honest at all times.

27

Being Envious of Others

*"It is in the character of very few men to honor
without envy a friend who has prospered."*
—AESCHYLUS

In Stephen Crane's classic novel, the main character en-
vies the "red badge of courage" on wounded soldiers.
Obviously, it is self-destructive to wish your body were
torn up like those of men dying on a battlefield. But it
can also be self-defeating to envy others their success,
status, luck, good looks or any other attribute.

For one thing, envy makes you feel ashamed. Most
of us like to think we can wish others well when they have
something we would like to have ourselves. When we
can't—and especially if we find ourselves wishing the
other person did *not* have what we want—we hate ourselves for being petty and self-centered. Also, dwelling
on what others have and we lack can turn into a self-
fulfilling prophecy: not only does it lessen us in our own
eyes, but few people want to be intimate with, or do business with, someone who constantly feels deprived. Finally, envy turns *good enough* into *not enough*. It makes
you feel the pain of deprivation even when you're not
actually deprived. And that sense of misfortune can reach

such proportions that it becomes impossible to feel contentment, satisfaction or gratitude, all of which are necessary ingredients for happiness. A life deprived of those qualities is desolate indeed.

Fortunately, envy is not a terminal disease. In my experience, one of the most effective ways to overcome it is to spend time with people who have the very things you crave. On the surface, this might seem odd. Isn't it easier to stave off envy by spending time with those who make you feel superior or fortunate by comparison? Yes, but it is only a temporary balm, whereas the other approach has curative power on two levels.

First, by associating with those you envy, you come to see the whole of their lives, not just the parts you covet. You might discover that they have flaws and weaknesses you never imagined, or an illness, a miserable marriage, an alienated child, a host of enemies. You might find that, along with the favors fate has handed them, they have had to endure challenges and hardships beyond anything you have experienced. You might even find that *they* envy *you*.

I witnessed a compelling example of this in a therapy group consisting of five women. One, Linda, was rich and beautiful. Although they tried to conceal it, the others envied her immensely, and it made her uncomfortable. One day, one of the women gushed over Linda's hairdo. "Here, it's yours," said Linda, and she whipped off her wig and tossed it to her shocked admirer. She had lost all her hair as a side effect of chemotherapy. In an instant, the women who wished they had what Linda had realized that Linda wished she did *not* have it.

"Who is rich? He who rejoices in his portion."
—THE TALMUD

The second reason to associate with those you envy is to learn from them. Like a uranium atom, envy contains energy that can be converted into either destructive or constructive forces. It can desolate or motivate. It can turn you into a complainer or a competitor. Envy creates a gap within you. If you wallow in that gap, you will fall further back. But if you fill the gap with constructive action, envy can drive you forward.

You can begin by identifying the qualities you need to have, and the actions you need to take, to obtain what you envy. Naturally, if what you envy is inherited wealth or natural good looks, or a stroke of luck such as winning a lottery, there is not much you can do about it. I suggest you accept the fact that biology and fate can be unfair. But if what you envy is, for example, success in a particular field, study those who have it. Find out how they attained it. Do they have skills, training or personal attributes you can acquire? Do they have a philosophy or a set of values you can adopt? Did they have a plan you can imitate? In my experience, people who are envied are not much different from the rest of us. Learning about them can help you feel "I can do that too" instead of "I wish I had that."

Before you can turn envy to action, you have to convert it to a more acceptable emotion. The first step is to get rid of any animosity you might feel. Stop wishing the other person did *not* have what you want—or hoping he or she will lose it. Then you can move to the next level: admiration. Learn to admire the person's achievement or good fortune without associating it with yourself at all. If you admire someone, you can let him or her have more without feeling you have less. Finally, move from admiration to emulation. By developing the qualities that made the person enviable, you'll become proud of yourself, and you can't feel pride *and* envy at the same time.

USABLE INSIGHT:
If you use it to fuel you, envy won't rule you.

TAKING ACTION

- As soon as you become aware of your envy, pause. Don't impulsively take an action or adopt an attitude that works against you.
- If you find yourself rooting against another person, remind yourself that you're not evil, you're just feeling deprived and are trying to lessen the pain in any way you can.
- Get to know the person you envy. Find out the truth of his or her life. You might find there is less to envy than you imagine.
- Try to appreciate and admire the person rather than wish you had what he or she has.
- Find out what qualities or skills enabled the person to attain what you envy.
- Figure out how you can emulate those qualities and skills and take constructive action toward making them your own.

28

Feeling Sorry for Yourself

"Sometimes I go about
In pity for myself
And all the while
A great wind is bearing me across the sky."
—*OJIBWA POEM*

"You can't wring your hands and roll up your
sleeves at the same time."
—*PAT SCHROEDER*

Melinda had spent seven years trying to make a difficult marriage succeed, only to see it shatter when her husband left her for another woman. Five years later she remained embittered. Despite my efforts to help her move in a positive direction, she spent most of her therapy sessions bemoaning her fate. She whined about how she had wasted the best years of her life, how she was forced to work at a dead-end job, how she was doomed to spend the rest of her life alone because no one wants a 40-year-old mother and all the good men were either gay or married anyway, and on and on.

"The excursion is the same when you go looking
for your sorrow as when you go looking
for your joy."
—*EUDORA WELTY*

Because she insisted on seeing it as half empty, Melinda's glass was getting drier and drier. She had convinced herself that it was impossible to be happy in her circumstances, and so, of course, she was miserable. It was only when she followed up on two suggestions that she was able to start turning things around. First, doing volunteer work at a battered women's shelter exposed her to troubles that made her own seem trivial by comparison. Second, at Divorce Anonymous she met women who had bounced back from situations just like hers. They understood what she was going through, but would not put up with self-pity. She could not dismiss their advice with "Easy for you to say," as she had with me and her married friends.

Feeling sorry for oneself has become a common affliction. If it's not an abandoned woman like Melinda, it's a couple who can't have children, a man who "coulda been a contender" if only he'd have gotten a break, or a worker who was laid off. It's grown children of alcoholics and victims of child abuse, or people whose parents neglected them, or overindulged them, or failed at being role models, or up and died on them. If it's not a childhood wound that brings on self-pity, it's a recent tragedy such as an illness, the death of a loved one or a financial setback. In some cases, it's an unchangeable personal characteristic, such as being fat or ugly or physically handicapped. Some people are chronic self-pitiers; they find new reasons to feel sorry for themselves whenever their circumstances change. You can recognize them because they start a lot of sentences with "If only . . ."

As a temporary device, self-sorrow can be comforting. As with an animal licking its wounds, it gives us a way to soothe our pain. It can also distract us from more wrenching emotions, such as grief or fear. And if we express it to others, self-pity can be a cry for help, a way to enlist sympathy or a means of getting ourselves off the hook—people don't expect much from those they feel sorry for.

But the benefits pale in comparison to the costs. For one thing, "Woe is me" is not compatible with hope. Feeling sorry for yourself consumes energy that could be used to turn your life around. As long as you're stuck in the past, you can't figure out how to create a better future. And while it might be comforting to gain the sympathy of others, they will eventually grow weary and lose respect for you. Then they will either avoid you or become cold, perhaps even hostile, when they're with you.

Self-pity feeds on itself. When you project a sorrowful image and a lack of faith, things tend to go wrong, which only gives you more reason to feel sorry for yourself. If the cycle continues long enough, you run the risk of appearing pathetic.

> *"Be content with what you have, rejoice in the way things are. When you realize there is nothing lacking, the whole world belongs to you."*
> —*LAO TZU*

If you fall into this self-defeating trap, the best hope is to seek out situations that will give you a new perspective. For example: spend time with people who are truly deserving of compassion; ask a friend to tell you honestly whether it bothers him to hear you complain about your situation; join a support group.

You need to make a 180-degree shift, from aggravation to appreciation, from grumbling to gratitude. Otherwise, your half-empty glass will empty completely.

USABLE INSIGHT:
If you keep feeling sorry for yourself, you'll really have a reason to be sorry.

TAKING ACTION

- Learn to recognize when you're feeling sorry for yourself.
- Realize that it's an enormous waste of time and energy, and a drain on other people.
- Do something for someone less fortunate than you. It not only makes you more aware of your own blessings, it makes you proud—and you can't feel pride and self-pity at the same time.
- List all the things in your life you feel grateful for.
- List everything that turned out better than you'd hoped.
- Identify someone who helped you in your life, and find a way to thank that person.
- If the reason you feel sorry for yourself is something shared by others, join a support group. Look for one that supports efforts to get past the problem and move on, not one that reinforces feelings of help-

lessness. In solution-oriented groups you will hear members not only sharing their pain but discussing hopes and plans for the future. If you have trouble finding the right group, express your desire to others; you might attract people who share your wish to get beyond the problem.

29

Assuming the Hard Way
Is the Right Way

"Seek not out the things that are too hard for thee, neither search the things that are above thy strength."
—THE APOCRYPHA

When Paul first came to see me, I assumed he was just another graduate student grappling with the excessive demands of his training. He was depressed and suffering from constant headaches and insomnia. He bristled at my suggestion that he take a sabbatical. "I'm not a quitter," he said. "I can take it, I just need some medication." In fact, he needed a total overhaul of his perspective.

As I got to know him, I realized Paul was different from other stressed-out students. For one thing, the goal of actually practicing architecture one day did not burn in his breast. Moreover, he had struggled throughout his undergraduate years with science and math—key disciplines for architects—and continued to work twice as hard as his classmates to grasp basic material. Why was he doing all this? Because he was raised to believe that nothing worthwhile came easily, that the only work deserving of the name was *hard* work. His father and mother had worked like dogs at their business, and his brother had worked equally hard to become a lawyer. Each time Paul thought of dropping out, he was gripped by shame and pushed himself even harder.

In discussing what Paul might do to relax a bit, I learned that he spent whatever spare time he had helping his former high-school basketball coach. He loved this and wished he had more time for it. It turned out that he had been merely proficient as a player, but his passion for the game, his grasp of its intricacies and his talent for motivating and teaching had marked him as an excellent coaching prospect. He had, in fact, been offered jobs. When I asked why he'd turned them down in favor of graduate school, his answer surprised me; it had nothing to do with status or money. It was because coaching young players was the most natural thing in the world to him. In his mind, that made it a hobby, not a vocation. Work was not something you were supposed to enjoy or find easy to do. It was supposed to be grueling. Otherwise, it would feel like cheating.

I told him that if he did not do something he loved, he would end up chronically depressed or burned out at an early age. I suggested he give serious thought to becoming a coach.

"But that would be the easy way out," he protested.

I countered with words that had once changed the course of my own life: "Sometimes the easy way out is the right way in."

Our society reveres hard work so much that we often consider ourselves lazy or escapist when we choose what is pleasurable or comfortable. When something comes too easily, we get suspicious; we feel there might be some hidden trap, as when we're asked a question whose answer seems obvious. "Is this a trick?" we wonder.

> *"There is nothing so easy but that it becomes difficult when you do it reluctantly."*
> —*PUBLIUS TERENTIUS AFER*

Such thinking can cause you to turn away from precisely those activities that would bring you the most fulfillment. Instead, you might take on something that feels like "real work," something tedious and difficult. Then, when you fail at that task, you berate yourself, thinking you're inadequate or that you don't know what you're doing. The real problem is that you don't *love*, or even *like*, what you're doing. The missing ingredient isn't skill or knowledge but enthusiasm. Sure, you can do things well even if you don't like doing them, but only for a short time. If you lack passion, even a minor obstacle or setback is enough to make you give up. But if you love what you're doing, you're likely to persist.

> *"Follow your bliss."*
> —*JOSEPH CAMPBELL*

I often see this with people who have difficulty delegating responsibility. Elaine was a successful entrepreneur who worked herself ragged because she insisted on dealing with administrative details she not only hated but found hard to do. She had a gift for people skills. Talking with clients and suppliers, charming and persuading them, came as naturally to her as walking. It was so easy, in fact, that she downplayed its importance. She felt she was not a legitimate businesswoman if she did not dive into the minutiae of management and finance. So, instead of delegating those responsibilities, she spent hours every day slogging through tasks she found laborious. This not only detracted from her real skills, it made her feel inadequate—since she did the job poorly—and guilty because she hated it so much she started cutting corners.

Next time you plunge into something that comes easily, remember that just because you're enjoying yourself does not mean you're not working hard—it only *feels* as though you're not. And don't let people convince you that you're foolish or lazy. They're probably jealous because they don't love what they're doing.

USABLE INSIGHT:
Sometimes the easy way out is the right way in.

TAKING ACTION

- If you are having fun and things are coming easily to you, don't feel guilty. It doesn't mean you're being irresponsible or lazy.
- Look for a way to turn what you enjoy into a meaningful pursuit or career.
- If you are plagued by frustration and doubt, consider the possibility that you are not doing something that comes easily and naturally to you.

30

Thinking "I'm Sorry" Is Enough

"Repent what's past; avoid what is to come."
—SHAKESPEARE

Some of the most touching moments in therapy occur when decent people confess to having betrayed, offended, or taken advantage of someone they care about. I recall, for example, a thick-skinned Hollywood agent who wept in my presence for the first and only time because she had gotten drunk and yelled at her ailing mother-in-law in a nursing home. Then there was the real estate developer who blubbered uncontrollably with remorse over a midlife fling that had left his wife devastated. In both instances it wasn't just the guilt and shame that was so upsetting, it was the agony of not knowing how to make things right.

"Apologizing—a very desperate habit—one that is rarely cured. Apology is only egotism wrong side out."
—OLIVER WENDELL HOLMES

Making amends is crucial in healing a wounded relationship; it is the only way we can demonstrate to others that the hurt we caused them matters to us. The problem is, we often don't know *how* to make amends, so we convince ourselves that time alone will heal the wound, or we mumble a quick apology that falls short of the mark. "I'm sorry" might suffice for minor injuries, but serious damage requires stronger medicine, and usually more than words. Otherwise, the people we hurt will continue to withhold their trust. This only frustrates us further. Then we'll get mad at them for not accepting our apology. "They won't let go of it," we'll complain, when in truth we haven't finished making amends.

> *"Don't make excuses—make good."*
> —*ELBERT HUBBARD*

The first step in correcting the situation is to understand that an injured party typically goes through three emotional stages, which I call the Three H's:

Stage 1: *Hurt.* The bubble of invulnerability has been burst; they now realize how badly they can be harmed.

Stage 2: *Hate.* They're enraged at the person who violated their trust and stole their feeling of safety.

Stage 3: *Hesitation.* They won't allow themselves to get close again until they feel safe.

If the hurt is severe, the most heartfelt words will fall on deaf ears; only a compensating action can replace the painful memory and enable the offended party to relax his or her guard. This can be accomplished by balancing the Three H's with the Three R's:

1. *Remorse.* You have to show that it hurts you to have hurt them. The best way is to state emphatically, "I

hurt you, didn't I?" Follow this with a simple, sincere statement that says: I know I was wrong, and I care about the pain I caused you. When someone is in pain, explanations are extraneous.

2. *Restitution.* For minor injuries, a simple gesture like sending flowers might suffice. But serious offenses might call for a public act of contrition. The agent who lost her temper in the nursing home apologized not only to her mother-in-law and her husband but to everyone who witnessed the scene. The adulterous developer used a simple but effective form of restitution: at my suggestion, he allowed his wife to let loose and vent her rage while he listened without answering back or defending himself.

3. *Rehabilitation.* To overcome the fear of being hurt again, the injured party needs more than promises; only a genuine change of behavior can restore faith and trust. For the agent, this meant participating in a program to stop drinking and demonstrating that she could act appropriately when irritated by her mother-in-law. The developer entered couples counseling with his wife and made an honest effort to resolve the frustration and discontent that had driven him to have an affair.

It often hurts more to be hurtful than to be hurt. With remorse, restitution and rehabilitation you can heal the pain of having hurt someone you love and at the same time show that you can be trusted. If you work consistently at the Three R's, the burden will eventually shift to the other person. At one point, he or she must be willing to drop the bitterness and give you a second chance. Without that act of faith, a wounded relationship can't begin to heal.

USABLE INSIGHT:
Love means always having to show you're sorry.

TAKING ACTION

- Try to feel the Three H's from the other's point of view. Consider:
    a. Why he might feel hurt.
    b. How and why he might hate you for hurting.
    c. Why he would hesitate to lower his guard and trust you again.

- Think of the Three R's *you* would need if you were in his shoes.
    a. What kind of remorse would it take to ease your hurt?
    b. What kind of penalty or restitution would it take to lessen your anger and hatred?
    c. What changes in behavior would it take for you to trust again?

- Let the person know you realize you were wrong and care about the pain you caused.
- Offer restitution by giving something that costs more than money.
- Make him feel safe by behaving in a nonhurtful way in similar situations.

31

Holding It All In

"Give sorrow words; the grief that does not speak
whispers the o'er-fraught heart and bids it break."
—SHAKESPEARE

I was once a guest expert on a Sally Jessy Raphael show in which the topic was family secrets. The guests were three women: one had watched her father kill her mother and then himself; one had been raped and impregnated by her brother; and one had been told as a child that her father was dead only to learn, as an adult, that he had been living in the same town all along.

I admired the courage it took these people to tell their stories to millions of strangers. Off camera, I remarked that it must have been hard to get them on the show. I was mistaken. They had actually written to request an appearance. They weren't merely attention-seekers. They desperately needed to purge themselves of secrets they had been carrying around for years, and they chose this show because they perceived Sally as trustworthy and her faceless viewers as no discernible threat. The sense of relief in those tortured souls was palpable.

The experience crystalized something I'd known for

some time: how important it is to talk about horrible experiences.

"Words are the physicians of a mind diseased."
—*AESCHYLUS*

After you experience something horrible, the obvious impact of pain, fear and loss is usually accompanied by another piercing feeling: loneliness. Even in a shared trauma such as a flood or an earthquake, the impact is uniquely felt by each individual, and to some extent everyone feels alone. For example, couples who lose a child usually grieve together but experience the tragedy in different ways. For the mother, the dominant feeling is usually loss; the object of her maternal love is gone. For the father, the overwhelming feeling is often shame—for having failed in his role as protector. Talking it out eases the sense of isolation; you feel more a part of the world instead of apart from it.

In addition, expressing yourself is a way of purging emotions. A horrible event leaves a toxic residue, and the act of describing it to another person serves as a syringe to draw out the accumulated poison. If you don't get rid of that poison, you will have to use defense mechanisms such as denial and repression to disconnect from the horror. The poison will accumulate until it pollutes your body, mind and soul, with potentially disastrous consequences.

The more quickly and more completely you express yourself, the faster and easier the healing. Letting it out early is the emotional equivalent of getting back on your bike after a fall. The longer you wait, the scarier it becomes. Also, the pain you suppress accumulates and gathers to it anything of a similar nature. The end result can be anything from a psychosomatic illness to a phobia.

Why, then, do we hold it in? Like all self-defeating behavior, it seems the more expedient choice. For one thing, we fear that letting it out will be overwhelming. After all, every time the memory pops into mind we feel pain, not relief. We assume that telling it to others will make matters worse. We're also afraid that if we unburden ourselves to the wrong person, we won't feel soothed at all. Rather, we'll only burden them and turn them off. Our feelings might be disregarded or trivialized, and we will be made to feel foolish. Another reason we hold our feelings in is that we are afraid we won't be able to stop at just remembering the pain but will relive it and become overwhelmed.

As a therapist I ask specific questions to encourage patients to describe terrible events in detail: What color was it? How loud were the sounds? Was it cold in the room? Could you smell anything? In a safe environment, reliving the incident through the senses brings out feelings that might have been suppressed. This can facilitate healing.

A good example is Gay, a single mother who ran a mail order business from her home. One day, caught up in her work, she inadvertently left her front door open. She was on the phone when she heard a loud screech of brakes, a scream and an awful thud. She ran out to find her child bleeding and unconscious as a hysterical driver tried to revive him. The child survived but was disfigured for life. Gripped by guilt and haunted by nightmares,

Gay found the memory too painful to discuss. After a while, though, she poured forth the entire gruesome story in precise detail, including what her child looked like in the street and how ashamed she felt in the emergency room. By spelling it all out, Gay was able to begin healing, and eventually to forgive herself.

> *"What soap is for the body, tears are*
> *for the soul."*
> —*JEWISH PROVERB*

Because they are trained to listen and required by law to honor confidentiality, therapists are often the best people to hear your tale. But they are not the only good listeners. Sometimes the best choice is someone who has experienced a similar horror. Such people are in the best position to say convincingly, "I understand," and "You're not alone." For that reason, a peer support group is often an indispensable adjunct to therapy.

Whatever their relation to you, good listeners have certain traits in common: they listen closely and patiently, without tuning you out; they accept your feelings without dismissing or trivializing them; and, perhaps most important, they are wise enough to validate that what you experienced was, in fact, horrible.

It is not enough merely to think about a terrible memory or vent your feelings to an indifferent ear. You cannot heal until you feel; you cannot feel until it is safe; and you cannot feel safe unless someone is willing to listen until the pain subsides.

USABLE INSIGHT:
Having the horror heard helps to heal the hurt.

TAKING ACTION

- Find an empathic person with whom you feel free to share your story.
- Ask for a green light to express yourself fully and without time restraints.
- Ask him or her to listen without judging, questioning or commenting on what you say.
- Describe your experience in as much detail as you can recall, including sights, sounds, tastes, smells and, most of all, feelings.

32

Quitting Too Soon

*"Perseverance . . . keeps honor bright: to have
done, is to hang quite out of fashion, like a rusty
mail in monumental mockery."*
—SHAKESPEARE

Paul was smart, charming and highly energetic, a man
with big ideas and the ability to get others excited about
them. He should have been a big success. But every one
of his ventures, like each of the jobs he'd taken, had ended
in disappointment. His wife, Ruth, was tired of it. She'd
been virtually supporting both of them for nine years.
"He just doesn't try hard enough," she complained.

In fact, Paul didn't need to try harder, he needed to
try differently. He would get wildly enthusiastic when
launching a new enterprise, only to get restless when it
came time for the detail work and frustrated by delays
and obstacles. If Paul were an athlete he'd jump out to a
big lead, then suffer a letdown while his opponent shot
ahead. He needed to learn what the CEO of a major cor-
poration once told me: "The key to success is tolerating
boredom." It requires revising, fine tuning, getting the
bugs out. If you get excited only by novelty, if you can't
tolerate the tedious part of the process, you'll lose pa-

tience and quit. That's what would happen to Paul. As soon as reality set in, the thrill would lessen, and he would decide that whatever he was striving for was wrong or futile. "It's not turning out the way I thought it would," he would say. Or, "This is not what I really want to do."

"Great works are performed not by strength but
by perseverance."
—SAMUEL JOHNSON

Boredom is not the only reason we quit too soon. When something, whether a job or a marriage, turns out to be more difficult than we anticipated, some of us decide it's not worth the effort. This is especially true when the obstacles we run into expose an area of weakness or inadequacy. The fear of humiliation shatters our willingness to persevere. We don't admit this to ourselves, of course. We just find reasons why it's best to cut our losses.

Like most self-defeating behavior, quitting serves a purpose. It relieves frustration and anxiety when we feel stuck or trapped. It keeps us from confronting a deeper fear—that we don't have what it takes to succeed, for example. It can also be a disguised cry for help or a way of asking for a pep talk. Men are especially prone to quitting as a matter of pride; to them, asking for help is the same as begging. That's why it takes 500,000 sperm cells to fertilize one egg: men are too proud to ask for directions.

"Effort is only effort when it begins to hurt."
—JOSÉ ORTEGA Y GASSETT

But the comfort of quitting exacts a steep price, and not just the obvious one, which is not reaching our goals. When we quit repeatedly, we lose credibility in others' eyes, and eventually in our own as well. No one respects a quitter. We also never learn the value of perseverance or the skills needed to work through obstacles and overcome frustration.

Of course, there are times when all the effort and good intentions in the world won't salvage the project or relationship. But there is a difference between stopping and quitting. Stopping implies reevaluating and adjusting your course of action. Quitting implies giving up, abandoning ship, releasing yourself from the burden of responsibility.

> *"Failure is not the falling down but the staying down."*
> —MARY PICKFORD

How can you tell the difference between quitting and a sensible decision to cut your losses? One way is to look at the past and get a sense of what your pattern is: have you been more likely to quit too soon, or to hold on too long? It also helps to get input from knowledgeable people. Use them to determine whether you've explored all the available options, gathered all the necessary information, solicited all the possible help. If you haven't, chances are you're quitting too soon.

You know the old saying, "If you can't stand the heat, get out of the kitchen." Well, if you always get out as soon as the kitchen gets hot, your life will end up half-baked.

USABLE INSIGHT:
You have more control over trying or quitting than
you do over succeeding or failing.

TAKING ACTION

- Think of the last time you quit something, and review the positive and negative consequences of having done so.
- Look at the present situation and write down the potential pluses and minuses of quitting at this time.
- Make a list of your other options, with the pluses and minuses of each one.
- Enlist the help of someone who can be objective and nonjudgmental in helping you evaluate the situation. (You might want to go through the previous two steps with that person.)
- If you're inclined to quit, ask yourself *why*, and why *now*. Are the reasons justifiable, or are you merely hoping to avoid something unpleasant, such as embarrassment or boredom?
- If you decide to hang in there, enlist the help and support of someone you can count on.

33

Letting Others Control Your Life

*"It is not easy to find happiness in ourselves, and
it is not possible to find it elsewhere."*
—AGNES REPPLIER

Fran, a 32-year-old paralegal who called herself "the
queen of the people-pleasers," gets credit for what I call
The Cheshire Cat Syndrome. She told me that she felt
like the feline creature from *Alice in Wonderland*, who
would alternate between visible and invisible while its
smile would always remain. Fran smiled through all her
relationships—with parents, bosses, friends and lovers—
but now, in therapy, her face was twisted with pain. "I've
become more and more invisible," she said. "I'm afraid
I'm going to disappear altogether, and I don't know how
to make it stop."

Like Fran, many people care so much about what
others think of them that they lose track of themselves.
It's as if the route to self-esteem passes through a toll
booth of other people's opinions, and each time they
drive through they pay with a piece of their identity.

Many of the adults I see in therapy are unable to
remember much about themselves in childhood, but they
remember other people quite vividly. They recall when

Mom and Dad seemed happy or sad, enthused or exhausted, cheerful or angry. This is because they learned, as children, that the way to feel safe was to do whatever made an angry dad smile or a depressed mom brighten—and how *not* to make them angry or depressed. Rather than focus on their own sense of vitality, initiative and growth, their efforts went into making their home calmer and less dangerous. As a result, their sense of worth was determined by what those they depended on felt about them: when their parents seemed happy they felt worthwhile; when their parents seemed unhappy they felt they were bad and somehow to blame.

> *"I have not moved from there to here without I*
> *think to please you, and still an everlasting*
> *funeral marches round your heart."*
> —ARTHUR MILLER

When too much concern with the desires, wishes and needs of others are carried into adulthood, you can develop a prove-show-hide-please personality. You spend much of your life trying to prove things to others, show them you're worthy, hide unpleasant truths from them and please them—all in an effort to feel safe and worthy.

When your motivation is to *prove* yourself to others, that is because you feel they don't believe *in* you. You think, "I'll prove I'm worthy of their faith." Whereas proving stems from a deep sense of hurt, *showing* is rooted in anger. It's a response to the perception that others don't believe you, period. Because you think they regard you as a phony or a liar, you constantly have to demonstrate your authenticity.

The impetus to *hide* comes from fear. Believing that another person is intolerant and unforgiving, you are wary of being attacked if you make a mistake. So you live a secret life, hidden from criticism but also from your true feelings and true personality. The motivation to *please* usually stems from the feeling that making someone happy is the ticket to being loved and accepted. You appease and pacify to create a cheerful environment, and when you fail you invariably feel guilty.

To a certain extent, most people in close relationships link their well-being to the moods of another person. The tragedy occurs when you become so consumed by proving, showing, hiding and pleasing that you relinquish control of your life, sacrificing your needs and desires on the altar of another. You might be able to rationalize living that way for a while, vowing to get back to your own life one day. But if you wait too long, you might find you have lost your way entirely.

USABLE INSIGHT:
You can't live for others without losing your self.

TAKING ACTION

- Determine to what extent you are a prove-show-hide-please personality by rating yourself on a scale of 0 to 10 on each of these characteristics. In your most important relationships, how much of your energy is devoted to proving yourself to others, where 0 equals none and 10 equals all? Once you have the answer, do the same for show, hide and please.

- If the sum of all four totals is more than 20, you are probably living more for others than yourself. You are squelching your own desires, interests and ambitions to make someone feel a certain way about you.

- Realize that you have very little power to make others happy and almost none to *keep* them happy.

- Tell the other person that he has done nothing wrong, but that you've realized you tend to defer to others more than is good for you.

- Tell him that from now on you plan to be honest about expressing disagreement and disappointment, and that you hope he will understand.

- Monitor your follow-through by rating yourself once a month, as in step one.

- Seek out people who do not expect you to be more to them than you are to yourself. You may not be attracted to them now, because you are drawn to what is familiar, namely people you can please and serve. But the familiar may not be good for you.

34

Leaving Too Much to Chance

*"Chiefly the mold of a man's fortune is in his
own hands."*
—FRANCIS BACON

For a therapist, it is almost an everyday occurrence to
hear someone say, "From now on it's going to be different" or "I'll never do that again." Sadly, it is also an
everyday occurrence to hear someone, sheepish and
downcast, say, "Nothing ever changes" or "I blew it
again."

Sometimes vows are made unthinkingly, simply because it feels good to make them. It enables us to pat
ourselves on the back for our good intentions—or to
make others feel better by assuring them that things will
be different in the future and they won't be hurt, let down
or offended again. In those cases, it is no surprise that
the vow has all the staying power of a campaign promise.
But more often than not our vows are sincerely made.
We mean what we say. We want the future to be different. We have every intention of changing. The problem
is, we leave things to chance, assuming that our good
intentions are enough to get the ball rolling and that we
can improvise from there.

"Hell is paved with good intentions."
—*ENGLISH PROVERB*

If you really want things to be different in the future, you have to know *how* to change. You need a plan. Otherwise, the future is likely to repeat the past—or be even worse. You might set change in motion, but, lacking the tools to follow through, end up biting off more than you can chew. Like nature as a whole, human nature abhors a vacuum. When faced with unfamiliar circumstances, you might feel unprepared and try to fill the vacuum with tried and true behavior that might not serve your new purpose. As a result, you can end up not only ashamed and disappointed but in real trouble.

I've seen it happen, for example, to hard-working men who are facing retirement. "I can't wait," they say, and reel off all the trips they'll take and the hobbies they'll indulge. But they fail to plan their finances properly and end up with only broken dreams to show for a lifetime of work. Others plan for the money but not the time. Asked what exactly they intend to do when they retire, they reply, "I'll worry about that when it happens. I'm looking forward to doing whatever the hell I want." Then the day comes, and they don't know what to do with themselves. They end up feeling useless and making everyone around them miserable. As the wife of one such man put it, "He wasn't well rounded when he was young and flexible, so how can he be now that he's old and rigid?"

I've also seen it happen to single women in their late thirties who hear the ticking of their biological clocks. They want to have a child so badly that they grab the first available opportunity, whether or not they've found a suitable partner. When asked how they will provide for the baby, how they hope to manage work and child care or afford a larger apartment, they appear certain that maternal love is strong enough to overcome any obstacle. A similar illusion affects lovers. Whether they're young Romeos and Juliets or middle-aged romantics who just know it's going to be different this time around, they follow their hearts without letting their heads consider the challenges of building a life with another person. Love conquers a lot, but it doesn't conquer all.

> *"He that waits upon fortune is never sure*
> *of a dinner."*
> —BENJAMIN FRANKLIN

Leaving too much to chance has dire consequences when what's at stake is a change of destructive behavior. Take, for example, a man who promises to stop battering his wife. Chastened, contrite, and possibly having been punished by the law, he might truly mean it. But without a plan—a commitment to therapy, an effort to resolve the causes of his discontent, a blueprint for responding nonviolently to conflict—he is likely to revert to his old impulses when his buttons are pushed.

Similarly, people who vow to give up smoking, drugs, alcohol or other destructive habits are doomed to fall off the wagon if they leave things to chance. It's not enough to declare, "I'll never overeat again," or "That's the last bet I'll ever make." Without a plan to deal with the impulse when it returns, you don't have much of a chance. People who go on crash diets, for example, lose a lot of weight quickly, but they seldom have a plan for *keeping* it off; hence, they end up fatter than ever. That is precisely why a program such as Alcoholics Anonymous works. It's a plan; it offers a way to stop and a way to enforce the follow-through.

> *"Chance is a word void of sense; nothing can*
> *exist without a cause."*
> —*VOLTAIRE*

In *Field of Dreams* the main character, played by Kevin Costner, heard a voice that said, "If you build it, he will come." He made a plan and stuck to it, and his deepest dreams came true. Wanting things to be different without a strategy for *making* them different will keep them the same. But if you plan it you can build it, and if you build it, it will come.

USABLE INSIGHT:
An ounce of planning is worth a pound of luck.

TAKING ACTION

- Start with the end in mind. Picture how you want things to be, clearly and specifically. Ask yourself what, when and where and form an image of that future in your mind's eye.
- Now ask how. Figure out exactly what you'll have to do to get there.
- If appropriate, break down your goal into segments.

What specific steps must you take to reach each objective?

- Double-check to make sure the plan is doable.
- Figure out what kind of help you'll need. Will you need experts? Money? Support or sacrifice from your family?
- Find a way to monitor your progress. Unless you periodically follow up, you might not follow through. One way to do this is to make your plan public; state your intentions to people you trust and ask them to hold you accountable.
- If you have an impulse to scrap the plan, resolve not to give in unless you have a plan for changing plans.

35

Letting Fear Run Your Life

"The only thing we have to fear is fear itself."
—FRANKLIN DELANO ROOSEVELT

*"You gain strength, courage and confidence by
every experience in which you really stop to look
fear in the face. You are able to say to yourself, 'I
lived through this horror. I can take the next
thing that comes along.'"*
—ELEANOR ROOSEVELT

Stan was a 52-year-old mechanical engineer at an aerospace company who drove forty miles to work each day. Then he had a car accident. After a short recuperation he was fine physically, but he remained injured mentally. He was terrified of driving. To preserve his job he braved it out as a car pool passenger, but rode white-knuckled all the way. The only driving he did was to drive other people crazy.

Ruth was a 43-year-old high school principal and mother of three. When she discovered that her husband Ted was having an affair, she went into a tailspin. Despite Ted's elaborate displays of remorse and his sincere efforts to work through the marital problems that contributed to his infidelity, Ruth could not overcome the paralyzing dread she felt whenever he was out of her sight. It got so bad that her own life came to a standstill.

What do Stan and Ruth have in common? They were both trauma victims who were terrified to the point of incapacity by the fear of a recurrence.

> *"Nothing in life is to be feared. It is only*
> *to be understood."*
> —*MARIE CURIE*

Traumas tend to hit with a one-two punch. The first blow shatters our innocence and sense of safety. The second is not a trauma at all, but the *fear* that whatever happened will happen again. A wall of terror goes up where trust once stood. With our essential vulnerability exposed, we feel that if the second shoe were to fall we would be irreversibly damaged and perhaps not even survive. This deep apprehension can lead to withdrawal. If it's exceptionally strong it can even turn into a phobia, the ultimate form of avoidance.

Tragically, the fear of a second trauma can be more devastating than the trauma itself. Ruth's anticipatory dread was so strong that if her husband, a surgeon, was too tired to make love she would assume he'd been with a mistress. She was so terrified of other women that she insisted that Ted stay away from social functions. She even examined his patient records to see what kind of women he'd been treating. After a while, Ruth's paranoia was a bigger threat to the marriage than Ted's affair.

The tendency to expect a second shoe to fall has its roots in early childhood. When a child has a trauma, such as diving into a pool and hitting bottom or falling off a bike, he or she feels unprotected. If the parents make too big a deal of the incident, the molehill becomes a mountain in the child's eyes: "Anything that upsets Mom and Dad that much must be truly awful, so I'd better not try it again." Conversely, if the parents treat the trauma too lightly, the child not only feels injured but alone. Psychologically, the aloneness can be more frightening than the injury. In either case, the net effect is to avoid picking oneself up and trying again. The emotional memory gets buried in the psyche. When, as adults, a fresh trauma retriggers the feeling, they protect themselves by constructing a psychological moat around themselves or becoming obsessed by the fear of a recurrence.

> *"To conquer fear is the beginning of wisdom."*
> —*BERTRAND RUSSELL*

Smart parents, on the other hand, comfort their traumatized kids, then encourage them to try again before the fear becomes debilitating. When the children do dive into the pool or get back on the bike without getting hurt, they learn that they are resilient. They also learn that if they stand up to fear and take action, the second shoe does not have to fall.

That is precisely what adults should do when they are traumatized. Only by getting on with life and taking positive action can we overcome the fear. In Stan's case, I convinced him to start driving again, first on small streets, then working his way up to avenues and boulevards before venturing onto the freeway. For Ruth the solution was to act as if she trusted her husband. She forced herself to wish him a good trip when he left town on business and to attend gatherings without clinging to him when-ever another woman was in sight. Once Ted proved him-self trustworthy, Ruth was able to trust him for real and get on with her life.

When you are wounded by the vicissitudes of life, it is normal to be scared. It is normal to be knocked off bal-ance. It is normal to want to shrink into a protective shell. But the sooner you resume living, the less likely you are to become a casualty. Action speaks louder than fear.

USABLE INSIGHT:
Feeling afraid does not mean you are in danger.

TAKING ACTION

- Realize that just because you feel vulnerable does not mean you're fragile. Admit that you feel afraid and resolve not to let the fear dominate your life.
- Accept the fact that certain events cannot be pre-dicted or prevented.
- Realize that apprehension and avoidance can be more damaging than whatever you're afraid of.
- Return to your normal routine as soon as possible. If you can't do it all at once, take small, incremental steps to normalcy.
- If needed, enlist the aid of a trusted person who will encourage you to do more than you think you can.
- Notice that each action you take reduces your fear. It is like a series of inoculations.
- Focus on your resilience. Remember that you sur-vived the trauma and realize that you will survive the next one as well.

36

Not Moving on After a Loss

"Grief is the agony of an instant; the indulgence
of grief the blunder of a life."
—BENJAMIN DISRAELI

Marie had suffered the worst loss a person can endure: the death of a child. Always a cataclysmic event, this one was especially devastating because Marie's grown daughter had been brutally murdered by a man whose advances she had rejected, and there was a chance the killer would go free. In addition, Marie had recently lost her mother and her own breast to cancer. She saw no reason to go on living.

Hoping to buy time, I got her to promise that she would not commit suicide before the killer was brought to justice. But other than coming to her therapy sessions, she did little except stare at her garden and her photographs of her daughter. Her husband and I urged her to get on with her life. "I can't go on until I get over this," she said.

"It's just the opposite," I replied. "Unless you go on with your life, you won't get over it." I explained that only by pushing herself into activities and building new memories would she be able to dilute the impact of the excruciating thoughts that hounded her day and night.

It is certainly appropriate to grieve, and there is no reason to pretend the grieving has ended just because a customary mourning period has passed. But if at some point you do not pick yourself up and get involved with life again, you can become a prisoner of the past, trapped in the hypnotic trance of ongoing grief. If that happens, the year in which you suffered your loss could turn out to be not only the worst year of your life but, in effect, the beginning of the end.

> *"The past is but the beginning of a beginning,*
> *and all that is and has been is but the*
> *twilight of the dawn."*
> —*H.G. WELLS*

People who suffer a great loss hesitate to go on for a number of reasons. They might have been so dependent on their loved one for their identity that they feel unable to function adequately alone. Or, they might feel comforted by having people feel sympathetic toward them. What they don't realize is that people will ultimately lose sympathy and start to avoid them. Another reason people cling to grief is to idealize the departed, thereby assuaging their guilt for any negative feelings they might still harbor. Then there is the belief that moving on would dishonor the deceased. But in all my years of working with dying patients I have never heard one say to a loved one, "Grieve for me forever" or "Please don't remarry." On the contrary, they invariably say things like, "Don't waste time mourning. Go on with your life. I want you to be happy." Finally, many mourners think there is no way life can be the same now, so why bother? But the goal is not to replace what cannot be replaced, or duplicate what cannot be duplicated, but simply to create opportunities for new memories.

One of the most difficult things to do—and one of the most important—is to create new memories in the very area of your life in which the loss was experienced. People who lose a spouse, for example, tend to get more involved in their work or spend more time with friends and children. While that is certainly better than isolation, it is not as constructive as dating. After an appropriate time of mourning, becoming intimate with another man or woman hastens the healing by building new memories in the area of the loss.

> *"The only cure for grief is action."*
> —*GEORGE HENRY LEWES*

Of course, the parallel does not have to be exact, and in some cases it can't be. A middle-aged woman such as Marie, for example, could not bear another child. However, she could direct her energy into an approximate area. Her daughter had represented, in part, someone to care for and help, someone who needed her. She felt a huge emptiness where her need to nurture had once flourished. So, at my urging, she did volunteer work at a hospital and joined a support group for parents of murdered children. Eventually, she took under her wing a distraught young woman whose husband had recently been killed. Extending herself to others in this way infused new energy into Marie. She became more assertive with officials prosecuting her daughter's killer, and participated in groups lobbying for victims' rights. Now, three years later, she has meaningful memories of life after her most devastating trauma.

When you suffer a severe loss, you have to accept the fact that life will never be the same. If you cannot let go of your loss, start building new memories and perhaps, in time, the loss will let go of you.

USABLE INSIGHT:
Leave the loss behind by building new memories.

TAKING ACTION

- Gradually compartmentalize your grief. If you've lost a loved one and turned your house into a mausoleum, turn it back into a home for the living. Create a room, if you must, with momentos of the deceased, or confine it to an album of pictures.
- Do the same process internally, by allowing less and less time per day to dwell on the past.
- Start to build new memories to dilute the intensity of the painful ones. Become involved in new projects, jobs and people.
- Instead of mere time-fillers, try to select meaningful activities that enhance your feeling of esteem and make you feel proud. For example, devote time to helping those less fortunate than you.
- Join a support group. Only fellow sufferers can say "I know how you feel" convincingly and ease the sense of aloneness.

37

Not Getting Out When the Getting Is Good

*"I have spent my days stringing and unstringing
my instrument while the song I came to sing
remains unsung."*
—RABINDRANATH TAGORE

A surprising number of patients come to me not when they're in a bad situation but after they get themselves out of one. They might have finally walked out of an unhappy or abusive marriage, quit a frustrating dead-end job, or stopped pouring time and energy into a losing venture. They should feel liberated and relieved. Instead, they are filled with confusion and regret. What do they regret? That they wasted so much time being miserable when they could have escaped sooner. Why are they confused? Because they can't figure out what took them so long to snap out of it.

There are any number of reasons people stay in bad situations too long. For one thing, staying put means not having to risk change; enduring familiar difficulties often seems more attractive than facing the unknown. What if they quit that frustrating job and don't find a better one, or leave a bad marriage and end up alone? It also absolves them of the responsibility of having to make a painful decision. "I can't bear the thought of hurting the person I love," many unhappy spouses have told me. The prospect of feeling guilty for breaking a vow and abandoning a partner is often enough to keep them hanging on.

They find ways to convince themselves it's wiser to stay. They tell themselves things will surely get better, that life is tough and it's foolish to think it will be any different if they change their circumstances. They resign themselves to the notion that they couldn't find a better spouse, job, house or whatever anyway, so they might as well try to be content with what they have.

> "I shall tell you a great secret, my friend. Do not
> wait for the last judgment. It takes place
> every day."
> —ALBERT CAMUS

But such rationalization exacts a tragic price. If you wait too long, it can quickly become too late. Your options might expire, and with them every opportunity to change for the better. You might also begin to believe that something is wrong with you. "I must not be doing enough," you think. "Maybe I should try harder." You end up asking more of yourself than is reasonable, or try to do more than your share when you're already doing enough and no amount of added effort will make a difference. Eventually, you start to feel that you're no longer running your own life. Your enthusiasm and zest erode. If you're lucky, something ironic happens: you become so unhappy and so resentful that the situation changes despite yourself, because your spouse can't stand it any more and leaves, or your boss gets fed up and fires you. But the more likely result is that you get burned out and start to feel old before your time.

Waiting too long can lead to catastrophe. One executive I know was uncomfortable about a new employee but considered him so promising that he kept him on— just long enough to be defrauded out of twenty thousand dollars. Another example is a 38-year-old woman whose biological clock was ticking louder and louder but who stayed with her fiancé in hopes he would change his mind about having children. "He'll come around," she told me with certainty. "He's great with kids, he's just into his career right now." She also reasoned that at her age she wasn't likely to find anyone else who fit the bill anyway. The last time I saw her, she was childless and about to turn 41.

> *"Life is its own journey, presupposes its own change and movement, and one tries to arrest them at one's eternal peril."*
> —LAURENS VAN DER POST

The itch to change should not be scratched willy-nilly, of course, or you risk another self-defeating behavior: quitting too soon. Look for the telltale signs that the itch is deep and serious. One is losing interest, enthusiasm and concentration—or, in the case of a love affair, passion. You might feel guilty for not trying hard enough, but the problem could be that your heart is no longer in it. Another clue is finding yourself fantasizing a lot, imagining yourself in a different job, for example, or with another lover. A strong indication that change is overdue is getting melancholy or depressed on certain occasions. Birthdays, New Year's Day, wedding anniversaries, the date you started your job—these are not only times of celebration but of taking stock. If at such times you feel a sense of stagnation as opposed to progress, if you think you're falling behind or that you're far from where you thought you'd be, give serious thought to making a change.

Diplomats say they prefer to deal with the enemy they know rather than the ally they don't know. However, it's sometimes wiser to face the unfamiliar. If you wait until you're burned out, you may burn all your bridges first.

USABLE INSIGHT:
Sometimes the grass is greener on the other side.

TAKING ACTION

- Make an honest assessment of your level of discontent, frustration and unhappiness.
- Ask yourself what you want your life to be like five years from now? Can you get there under present conditions?
- Examine realistically the likelihood that the situation will change. What are the chances it will become more satisfactory? Is there anything you can do to bring that about?
- Ask yourself how bad would you feel if you knew things would never get better.

- Examine your options to see if there are viable alternatives to the status quo. Have you checked with experts? Talked to people who have made a similar change?
- Analyze the risks of leaving. How do they measure up to the consequences of staying?
- If you decide it's best to change, make a concrete plan and set it in motion, resolving not to be dissuaded by fear or guilt.

38

Not Asking for What You Need

*"Ask, and ye shall receive, that your joy
may be full."*
—GOSPEL ACCORDING TO JOHN

*"To live happily with other people one should ask
of them only what they can give."*
—TRISTAN BERNARD

Each year since their marriage fourteen years earlier,
Wendy and Jack Forrestal had spent Christmas week in
the same Palm Springs resort. The ritual spanned good
times and bad, health and sickness and the raising of two
children. For the previous five years, however, each of
them had hated it. Each was bored. Each had a yen for
change. And neither one said, "Can we go someplace else
this year?" Instead, on the assumption that the other
would consider it forbidden to break the tradition, they
pretended to have a good time.

For the Forrestals, the stakes were relatively small
and the consequences minor. That is not always so when
we fail to ask for what we need or want. The desire might
be something as mundane as a ride to the airport, but the

consequences of not asking for it explicitly can be profound. Take this typical situation, for example: Ozzie drops a hint, hoping it will get him what he wants without his having to put himself on the line. "Gee, I have to get to the airport by seven," he says. His frustration mounts as he waits for Harriet to offer a ride. By the time he has to call a cab, he's angry. In his mind, he's tallied all the favors he's done for Harriet and has concluded that she's selfish and inconsiderate. The atmosphere has become tense, and Harriet hasn't the faintest idea why. If she did know why, she could justifiably protest, "Why the hell didn't you say you wanted a ride?" Such misunderstandings can jeopardize a friendship.

More poignant, and far more devastating, are the deeper needs that go unmentioned. For example, many aging parents refrain from asking their children for help because they are afraid of scaring them away or being shunted into a nursing home—or because they feel guilty dragging their busy kids away from their own families. Then an emergency arises and their children, instead of simply doing what's necessary, roar, "Why didn't you tell me?"

In no area is this self-defeating behavior better exemplified, or more controversial, than in bed. Despite the flood of advice in magazines and self-help books, asking for what we need sexually remains a highly charged area. It takes courage and trust to ask for it, and a strong soul to listen. Where sex is concerned, our egos are so delicate that instead of hearing a request we are likely to hear criticism; if they have to ask, we figure, then we must be doing something wrong. The one with the need has to decide which is the bigger risk: the frustration of waiting for the partner to figure out what we want (or *don't* want), or possibly hurting his or her feelings by asking for it.

Whether your need is essential or trivial, before you learn to ask for it you have to overcome the pressure to keep quiet. We hold back from asking for what we want for very good reasons:

1. We don't want to hurt or offend the other person.

2. It helps us deny our neediness. Men are especially likely to view needing something as a sign of weakness—and to equate asking for it with begging.

3. It creates an inner sense of deservedness. Whether we realize it or not, most of us keep score of what we give and receive. Keeping our desires to ourselves lets us feel generous and noble—and to build accounts receivable for the future.

4. We might be asked for something in return. We're afraid if we get what we ask for we'll have an account payable, and the other person might take advantage.

5. We don't want to risk being refused. When I ask patients why they don't ask for what they need, they often say, "I wouldn't know what to do if I was refused." They're afraid they might do something destructive, or that the relationship might shift from one that deprives to one that's over.

6. We think we shouldn't have to ask for it. This illusion reflects a childlike wish to be totally known by another person. We want someone to anticipate our every need and fulfill it, just as parents did when we were infants.

The dilemma is, waiting for people to give you what you need is a terrific way to not get it. And while you're waiting, a number of problems are likely to develop. Feeling deprived as you nurse your unmet need, you can get moody, cold and sullen. You can end up resentful, thinking others know damn well what you need but just don't want to give it to you. Also, the temptation to fill the gap in some other way can build, leading to foolish behavior, or, in the worst cases, to the kind of compulsion—abusing alcohol or drugs, having affairs, gambling, and so on—that only adds shame and guilt to the feeling of deprivation.

It's not weak to ask for what you need. Nor is it selfish or offensive, as long as what you ask for is fair, reasonable and deserved. And it's not unnecessary. Indeed, asking might be the only way you'll get it, and just because you can live without it now doesn't mean you'll always be able to.

USABLE INSIGHT:
You don't have to ask for what you need as long as you don't mind not getting it.

TAKING ACTION

- Accept that you have needs. We all do, and eventually they come out.
- Whatever your need, determine whether or not you can live without it. Some needs are worth sacrificing for the sake of a relationship. But if doing without it

bothers you, and you find yourself fantasizing about having it, the need is probably too strong to ignore.

- Realize that if you don't ask for what you need, there is a good chance the other person won't know you need it. Few of us are mind readers.

- Try to request what you need without demanding, criticizing or complaining.

- State what you need as a fact. Express it as something you'd like to have from now on, as opposed to focusing on what you haven't been getting.

- Try to give the other person the option of saying yes or no. It's okay to hope he says yes, but try not to insist on it.

- Timing is important. If, for example, you want something sexual, don't ask for it when you're in bed. Instead, make it part of the prelude to lovemaking, as in, "You know what I'd like to do when you get home tonight?" Or, while watching a sexy movie or reading a book, say, "I'd like to try that sometime."

39

Giving Advice When They Want Something Else

"The first duty of love is to listen."
—PAUL TILLICH

Elizabeth storms into the house and lets loose. "You won't believe what happened," she roars. "I slaved on that proposal for weeks, and he makes the presentation himself. Doesn't acknowledge me. Doesn't even thank me in private!"

While she rants on, her husband Dave squirms in his easy chair, trying to think of the magic words that would calm her down. Finally, he interjects, "For God's sake, Liz, you're overreacting."

"Overreacting! I deserve some respect from him, not . . ."

"Why do you let him get to you?"

"Thanks a lot. I don't know why I bother to tell you these things."

You know what happens next. What began with Elizabeth's need to express her feelings turns into a bitter argument. It happens in most relationships. One party turns to the other for sympathy and support, but instead has her feelings trivialized. Then she ends up angry at the very person to whom she turned for understanding.

> *"Who cannot give good counsel? 'Tis cheap, it costs them nothing."*
> —ROBERT BURTON

This type of interaction occurs when we don't know how to deal with someone else's highly charged feelings. We want to make them feel better, to calm them down and help them get over whatever upset them. In the heat of the moment, what seems most expedient is to try to fix things. We jump in with what we think are clearheaded solutions: "Okay, let's take a look at your options," or "I told you you should quit that job." Or, we try to fix things by changing the person's feelings: "Hey, don't take it so seriously." "I'm sure he didn't mean it, don't let it bother you." Worse, we belittle the situation by saying something like, "Hey, just be glad you *have* a job," or "You think that's bad. Did I ever tell you about the time . . . ?" The intention may be to soothe, but such remarks come across as condescending and insensitive. What the other person hears is, "You're foolish to feel this way."

> *"Caring is the greatest thing, caring matters most."*
> —FRIEDRICH VON HUGEL

Such situations are especially delicate when they occur between parents and children. Steve and Tina Robinson came to see me about their daughter Nancy. A bright, charming 9-year-old, Nancy had begun to have trouble with other children. She had been acting belligerent, impatient and intolerant, and as a result was losing friends. When her parents learned what had been going on, they tried to talk to her. They gave her excellent advice about the importance of friendship and the consequences of treating people badly. Nancy's response was to become moody and sullen. The Robinsons kept trying, but their efforts were met with angry outbursts.

In my office, I asked Nancy what had been bothering her. "Nothing," she replied. I asked a few more times, using different words, and finally she said, "I don't know." I persisted gently, adding, "There must be something wrong, because you're such a good kid." She repeated that she didn't know, but clearly she was trying to figure out the answer. Then, after a quiet pause, she blurted out, "I was the first to be born, so I'll be the first to die," and she began to sob.

It turns out that Nancy's change of behavior had begun when her brother was born. The usual difficulty of adjusting to new siblings had been compounded by the connection she made between being older and dying first, and then by feeling alone with her fears. Her parents had responded with advice and guidance, but since neither were firstborn, like Nancy, they couldn't appreciate her special angst. What she needed was for someone to be patient and persistent in helping her find a way to express what she had been feeling.

When people are upset, there are usually two components: they are frustrated by the situation itself and they feel alone. We don't realize this because what we hear is, "I have a problem." It sounds as if they're asking for help, so we respond by offering advice. But often what they want first and foremost is simply to feel less alone. They want to see that you care. If you try to fix things without first acknowledging and empathizing with their anguish, it appears to them that you're being clinical, distant and intellectual, that you're simply trying to avoid their pain.

The central problem is, you're responding to something emotional with something logical. They want comfort and concern. If you offer only a solution, they might hear, "The fact that you're upset or hurt doesn't matter to me." It's as if you were saying, "Take two aspirin and don't call me in the morning."

When people you care about are upset, before you offer solutions, show them that you care. If you don't, the anger they already feel will turn on you. They'll get it off their chest and it will land on your face. "You don't understand," they snap. "Of course I understand," you reply. "This is what you should do about it." Or, they accuse you of not caring, and you respond with, "What do you mean, I don't care? Why would I give you a solution if I didn't care?" By then an energy transfer has taken place: you're angry and they've calmed down.

Let them know it's okay to feel whatever they feel and that you empathize: "Gee, if that happened to me I'd be angry too," or "I'd hate it if that happened," or "I was in a situation like that once. It was awful." If you do this, they will immediately feel less alone.

Then take it a step further: help them finish feeling their feelings. Asking leading questions such as "How bad does it feel?" is an excellent way to encourage them to talk it out. Once they do, they will calm down, and a more constructive discussion can follow.

USABLE INSIGHT:
People don't care how much you know until they know how much you care.

TAKING ACTION

- Show that you care about how someone feels by letting him fully express his emotions without censoring, judging or interrupting.
- If you sense that he needs to talk but is reticent, follow up by asking who, what, when, why and where questions.
- If he still hasn't gotten it all out, help him go deeper by asking questions such as "How bad does it feel?" or "How scared are you?"
- If the reply is vague, press him gently until he qualifies the answer with something like, "I feel like I want to die" or "I'm so terrified I can't sleep."
- As a general rule, don't offer advice unless he asks for it. If you're not sure whether he wants advice, ask if he would like some help or suggestions.

40

Backing Down Because You Don't Feel Ready

"Nerves provide me with energy. They work for me. It's when I don't have them, when I feel at ease, that I get worried."
—MIKE NICHOLS

"Doubt is not a pleasant condition, but certainty is an absurd one."
—VOLTAIRE

Paul was a criminal attorney who, at age 50, was on the brink of burnout. Tired of the stress, tired of office politics, tired of commuting, tired of nightmares in which defendants he helped set free did monstrous things, he decided to take a sabbatical and then open a small private practice near his home. The plan would entail financial risk, but he felt it could work if his family agreed to some downscaling.

To Paul's relief, his wife and children supported his decision, and they held firm when the time came to give notice to his company. But Paul himself suddenly became apprehensive. He was on the verge of backing down when he came to see me. "I'm scared out of my mind," he said. "Maybe I'm making a huge mistake. Maybe I'm just not ready for this."

Paul suffered from a misunderstanding many of us have before we make a significant change or start a new undertaking. He assumed that feeling uncomfortable equalled not being ready.

Whether what we're about to do is commit to a relationship, start a new career, have children or speak our mind to someone, we often expect to feel an imperturbable readiness, a mythical state of mind that knows no tension, no queasiness, no hesitation, no doubt. When, instead, we feel uneasy, we take it as a sign that we are not truly ready. Giving in to that feeling can be disastrous. When we look back on our lives, we regret not what we did but what we wanted to do and didn't.

In fact, when we face a challenge or a substantial change, it is normal to feel a sense of anxiety. It is normal for thoughts such as "Can I handle this?" or "Am I doing the right thing?" to cross our minds. If we cave in to such thoughts we end up settling for less than we deserve. If, instead, we accept that a certain degree of tension is necessary to keep our minds and senses alert, we can rise to the occasion and respond effectively to whatever comes along. In real life, as opposed to the movies, even heroes feel a certain jangling of the nerves before they save the day. World-famous athletes and actors have butterflies before performing. But they are not only used to it, they have learned to convert their nervous energy to motivation and effective action.

This anxious edge should not be confused with panic. Panic shuts us down. It is debilitating. It renders us ineffective and unresponsive. Had Paul been in a state of panic, I would have agreed that he was not ready. I would also have agreed if his plan had been unrealistic. If he'd said he was going to quit his job, use all his savings to buy a camper and support his family as an itinerant musician, I'd have agreed that his sense of unease should be heeded. But he had developed a sensible course of action to solve a genuine problem. His anxiety was perfectly appropriate for a responsible family man embarking on a major change.

Another distinction worth noting is between being ready and being prepared. Being ready means having sufficient resources to handle any reasonable contingency. Being prepared means having what is necessary for a specific occasion. For example, I feel ready to answer virtually any question about divorce because I have spent thousands of hours with patients who were going through the process. But, despite my experience, I would not be prepared to deliver a good lecture on divorce to my psychiatry students unless I had written and rehearsed one. Someone with far less expertise than I could memorize and deliver a perfectly good speech. He would be *prepared* to lecture, but he would not necessarily be *ready* to answer questions or advise someone who was going through a divorce.

The apprehension you feel might signal a lack of preparedness, not a lack of readiness. If that is the case, you can appease your anxiety with thorough preparation. But don't expect to eliminate all doubts and jittery nerves. That sort of thinking leads to what I call the zero-risk fallacy: you want a guarantee that nothing troublesome or unexpected will come up once you get going. There are no such guarantees in life. There is always uncertainty, especially when you're dealing with other human beings. That's why married people always chuckle when a young soon-to-be bride or groom gets cold feet. They know that she or he has been hoping for some divine sign to appear and erase every nagging doubt before the wedding—a romantic, but not quite realistic, wish.

The challenge is not to eliminate discomfort, but to recognize when you are as ready as you will ever be. If you wait until you are perfectly at ease, you may wait so long that life will pass you by.

USABLE INSIGHT:
Just because you're nervous doesn't mean you're not ready.

TAKING ACTION

- If you're tempted to back off because you don't feel ready, pause.
- Ask yourself why you believe you're not ready. List all the reasons.
- Ask yourself what would have to take place for you to feel ready.
- Ask yourself what the chances are that those prerequisites will come to pass. What would you have to do to make them happen? Is it worth the time and effort?
- Ask yourself whether or not you're prepared. To

shed an objective light on the question, ask people with experience what it takes to be prepared.

- Think of situations in the past where you have backed down. In retrospect, did those turn out to be wise decisions or ones you came to regret?

A Note to the Reader

As part of my ongoing research, I would appreciate hearing about your experiences with self-defeating behavior. Please let me know which behaviors concern you most and how they have influenced your life. Tell me what you've done to overcome them, and how the ideas and advice in this book have affected you. By sharing with me your victories and setbacks, ideas and suggestions, you will not only help me help others, but you will also help yourself. Formulating your thoughts in writing will add to your understanding and make you more aware of your feelings.

In addition, I would like to hear about self-defeating behaviors that are not covered in this book. Human beings invent just as many ways to sabotage their lives as to improve them. If you have poignant or humorous stories about self-defeating behavior (your own or others'), please share them with me.

You may write or email me at:

Mark Goulston, M.D.
1150 Yale Street, #3,
Santa Monica, CA 90403
mgoulsto@ucla.edu

About the Authors

MARK GOULSTON, M.D., a board-certified psychiatrist, was trained at Berkeley, Boston University, the Menninger Foundation, and UCLA, where he is an Assistant Clinical Professor at the Neuropsychiatric Institute. Dr. Goulston has appeared on local and national television, inluding *Oprah*, *Today*, *Leeza*, *Sally Jesse Raphael*, and *NBC News*. He is interviewed on radio two to three times per week, including *Jim Bohannan*, *Talk America*, and KFWB, Los Angeles. He has been profiled and quoted in magazines and newspapers frequently, including the *Los Angeles Times*, *Men's Fitness*, *Bottom Line Personal*, *the Wall Street Journal*, and *Ladies' Home Journal*. He contributes regular columns to the *Los Angeles Business Journal*, the *Aspen Daily News*, and is syndicated to college newspapers via the Chicago Tribune Syndicate. He has been an online consultant for Time Inc.'s ParentTime, iVillage, Yahoo!, and is currently the relationship advisor for lifescape.com.

PHILIP GOLDBERG is the author or coauthor of many books including *Get Out of Your Own Way*, (with Mark Goulston), *Passion Play* (with Felice Dunas), *Pain Remedies* (with the Editors of *Prevention* magazine), *The Intuitive Edge* and *Making Peace with Your Past* (with Harold Bloomfield).

Mark Goulston and Philip Goldberg are also the authors of *The Six Secrets of Lasting Relationships*.